# BREAKTHROUGH

SHATTER THE 25 LITTLE LIES HOLDING YOU
BACK FROM FIRING YOUR BOSS AND
LAUNCHING THE ONLINE BUSINESS YOU'VE
ALWAYS DREAMED OF

## JONATHAN GREEN

*Edited by*
ALICE FOGLIATA

SERVE NO MASTER: BOOK 5

Paperback ISBN: 978-1796215953

Hardback ISBN: 978-1947667204

# CONTENTS

# CONTENTS

# FOREWORD

Ever heard of free solo climbing? It's climbing without any ropes or equipment whatsoever. It's just a human being in climbing shoes with a bag of chalk on a wall. Death below.

Alex Honnold is the world's most accomplished free solo climber, now famous for climbing El Capitan—a 3,200-foot sheer granite wall—without ropes. Most spend multiple days and nights schlepping their way up El Capitan to finally reach the summit. Alex scurried up in a matter of hours.

Three hours and 56 minutes to be exact.

By some measures, if not most, this could be the greatest physical feat a human being has ever achieved.

How did he do it? He did it by existing as a singularly obsessed homeless vagabond, living out of a sweat, mildew, and ramen-scented van, near penniless, focused on one thing and one thing only—climbing. After 22 total years of honing his craft, with a relentless push towards meticulous perfection, he was able to comfortably and confidently shock the world.

Living "in a van down by the river" is the quintessential portrait of failure. Yet, most of us feel inspired about not just what Alex accomplished but also how he was able to remove the typical obstacles in life to follow his calling with little to no regard for the outcome. In the end, something extraordinary came of it.

Joe Rogan and Alex briefly discussed this on Joe's podcast in late 2018:

**Joe:** *Most people look at the path that the average person takes in life, you know—I wanna sell cars, I wanna be an insurance guy—and they look at it like it's death. They look at a kid—a young kid—who's like enjoying playing with his friends, doing sports, playing video games or reading comic books, and then you look at what could be the average path that the average person takes in life—sitting in an office all day and fluorescent lights... and it looks like death. It looks like a slow, aching death. But then I look at someone like you, and I'm like, "Wow." This guy is living a special life.*

**Alex:** *Ideally though someone would look at it and see that this is somebody living a very intentional life or having chosen a certain path. I would love to inspire people to live an intentional life that they care about. I don't necessarily feel like people all need to go free soloing.*

Living an "intentional life" is what Jonathan Green's book *Breakthrough* is all about. Jonathan lives an intentional life.

He carved his own, unique path in line with his vision of paradise. His intent in writing this book is to hand you a machete and the confidence and determination you need to use it to cut through the thick jungle of nonsense that stands between your current life and the one you aspire to live—that "special" life that nags at you from week to week, month to month, and year to year.

Much of the book revolves around something a little more achievable than accomplishing superhuman feats of skill, strength, courage, and endurance and having movies made about you like Alex Honnold. It focuses primarily on creating passive income streams and achieving true financial security and liberation for yourself and your family as a result.

Why? Because most of us are way beyond the stage of life where we can drop everything and focus on getting really good at something for 22 years without pay! Before we can live our inspiring, intentional lives—crafted to our own deep desires and visions—we must first increase our incomes, unburden ourselves from debt and decrease the number of hours of unwanted work that we have to do to as close to zero as possible.

Is such a thing possible? Yes, of course it is. And here's a big secret about achieving it: it's not harder or more time-consuming or expensive to learn than any other career path. It just has to be your focus. Study it, do it, taste a little success, taste a little failure and continually refine your approach until you've got it.

It won't happen all at once. I'm in my thirteenth year of

pursuing 100 percent passive financial freedom. I'm currently on day 78 of a 365-day trip. I still have to work two hours a day on average. Just because I'm not all the way there doesn't mean I haven't improved my life. It's pretty great. I haven't "gone to work" in eight years now.

It happened for me because I made it my focus. Instead of putting my effort into becoming a lawyer, a nurse or an engineer, I chose—because I love to travel—to figure out how to come back from a trip with more money than I had when I left. Simple as that. It took me four years to get there, and it could have been just a year if I knew what I know now—and actually believed I could achieve it. I spent the first three years wondering if I could even do it! How many years have you been wondering whether or not you could do it, too? How many books and courses have you bought? Certainly this isn't the first.

But this could be and should be your *last*.

Because this is not just a book. What Jonathan has created is so much more. It's a workbook. A course. A complete, thorough life-overhauling program.

*If you treat it as such.*

My advice, after being one of the first to read it, is to immediately shift your thinking about what you just purchased.

It's not a book to be browsed through and pondered!

And it's not *a* book. It's *the* book. It's the one you need. There is no need to look for others. Dedicate your all to it. Make it your Bible.

You'll need a notebook. You'll need ten to a hundredfold the amount of time and effort to complete this program than it will take you to simply read the words. Be ready for that. Don't treat it like a collection of pages.

With that attitude towards it, you'll get everything you could ever dream out of *Breakthrough* and more. You'll be well on your way to living an intentional life and watching the "slow, aching death" you're currently living gradually disappear in the rearview mirror. In time, you too may be able to free solo your own El Capitan.

Matt Stone (aka Buck Flogging)
www.QuitN6.com

# FREE GIFT

Thank you for your purchase of BREAKTHROUGH. There is nothing more important to me than your success. For that reason, I have created the Breakthrough Workbook.

This is a guide companion to this book that you can print out and work through side-by-side with this book.

You will find that taking notes and using this workbook will accelerate your results and get you to the success you deserve faster.

and click the link below to get instant access:

ServeNoMaster.com/break

# INTRODUCTION

"You're fired. Hand over your keys and any other company property and get out of here!"

These words, dripping with disdain, would be the last words any boss would ever say to me. Walking to my car with my head hung down, one of the best weekends of my life shattered into the worst. Friday, I signed a new lease on an apartment. Saturday, I bought a new car. And Monday, I was fired from my dream job after just thirteen days.

Everything I'd built toward for the previous decade was ripped right out of my hands. All my preparations, planning strategies, efforts, and education had suddenly become irrelevant. The system I'd put so much trust in had stabbed me in the heart.

I'd love to say that I stood and fought – that I took my boss to court because the way she fired me was illegal. But I didn't. In more than a decade of working for different bosses, I've learned one thing: most of them will do whatever they can get away with.

Driving home that Monday morning, there was a blizzard. The roads were covered in ice. It had been treacherous even to make it into the office that day. I thought my employers would appreciate the extra effort I put in, with so many other people calling in to take the day off. But they caught me by surprise and forced me to drive back home in that same blizzard.

Looking through my office window from the outside one final time, I saw my boss and her boss rubbing their hands together with glee, having removed me from their fiefdom. In that moment, I realized I was left with two choices. I could be shattered against the rocks, trying to find a lesser job to make ends meet and put things together, or I could accept my fate and grab the wheel of the foundering ship.

## 1

# ENEMY AT THE GATES

E very one of us has been in one of those situations where you felt powerless, and if you haven't, there's probably one coming your way. Something outside of your control puts you in a precarious financial situation – a boss firing you or an insurance company betraying you – and you don't know what to do. Suddenly, all of those premiums you paid mean nothing.

Just last year, my eighteen-month-old son required surgery. Despite the insurance claim being pre-approved, after six months of delays, with the underwriter and the insurance blaming each other, my claim was denied. That could best be described as dishonest. The difference between now and that blizzard morning is that I no longer depend on anyone else to take care of my family.

Whether you know it or not, the enemies are at the gates of your life right now. Just because you don't hear the gate rattling, doesn't mean they aren't there. Most Americans are one tragedy away from losing their homes.[1] It doesn't matter how important your job is or how much money you make. If you have a single source of income, that source of income can disappear in a snap of the fingers, and it doesn't have to be your fault.

The idea that your boss cares about you is a lie. It doesn't matter how educated you are, how much money you make, or how many barbecues you've been to with your boss. When push comes to shove, if the company says it's either your boss's job or yours, your boss will slide that knife between your ribs without shedding a single tear.

We live in a mercenary society.

Unfortunately, many of us don't realize that until it's too late. We believe that the camaraderie we form at work is something real that will last outside the workplace, but if you were to walk out of your office tomorrow and say, "Who's with me?" nobody would even look you in the eyes as you walk out alone with your head hanging in shame trying to hide your tears of disappointment.

There is a financial reckoning coming, and it comes for everyone. It can come in the form of a medical emergency. It can come in the form of you losing your job because of something your boss did. It could have nothing to do with you. Some of the biggest companies in the world had to go through massive swathes of layoffs because the boss was protecting himself. Before a boss takes a pay cut, he'll try to cut the staff by 10 or 20 percent.

It doesn't matter if your business is considered an institution. How many newspapers are now blogs?[2] How many of the largest companies in the world have disappeared and faded away from memory? It happens all the time. Every ten years, the economy cycles down. And somehow, no one ever sees it coming. But whether it's a savings and loans crisis, a junk bond scandal, a recession, an economic downturn, or the housing market goes down because those at the top were selling bad mortgages to everyone else, they get handouts from the government because they're too big to fail. You know who never gets that handout? People like you and me.

Times are even more precarious for those of us preparing for retirement. So many of us were led to believe that our 401ks and social security would be enough to support us through our twilight years. But who wants to live on a "fixed income" at the mercy of whoever is in office or running your retirement fund? Most people hit retirement age and aren't even close to where they need to be financially to survive. When you add in the increasing costs of everything from medicine to fuel, that monthly stipend that seemed great when you started your job a few decades ago feels like a pittance now. It's probably not enough.

It's time to stop relying on some external force to take care of you.

The government, the rich, and the politicians are not going to save you because they don't care about you. Regardless of what political party you're from, what your affiliation is, or how much you've donated to someone's campaign, when it's you or them, you will get the knife.

The enemy is coming for you, and they're already at the gates. They are banging on your front door looking for a way to get into your house and destroy you.

But the good news is that it's not too late. The door has not been breached. Together, we're going to develop a plan to prepare you for the day the enemy gets in. I still hope that day never comes for you – maybe you're one of the few people who never miss a mortgage payment, don't have any credit card debt and aren't paying off a student loan in their thirties or forties. You may be one of the lucky 1 percent of Americans who have no debt in their lives. If so, that's wonderful. But if you don't have a plan for the day you lose your job, then you won't survive.

On this journey together, we're going to learn how to break through every single barrier that's been holding you back from starting your own business, opening your own revenue streams, and protecting yourself from economic shocks.

By the time you finish reading this book, you're going to have a deep understanding of how you can set up financial systems that will protect you from the unexpected. We are going to develop an action plan that you can implement starting today to prepare for that rainy day. Winter is coming, but it doesn't have to destroy you.

I don't know which enemy will breach your defenses, but I know how to prepare you for all of them. Whether it's losing your job, getting crushed by debt, or an economic downturn, you can create alternative revenue streams that will protect you and your family and ensure that you can have a prosperous future.

# WHO THE DEVIL ARE YOU?

There's a good chance that you bought this book because the cover looks awesome, the title sounds interesting, and the advertising campaign we put together was dazzling - you were pulled in by that excitement. But that shouldn't be enough to get you to read the rest of this book. Don't ever take knowledge unless you know who it's coming from.

In my life, I've received so much bad advice from people who didn't even know what they were talking about. Most people would rather give you advice than admit they're unqualified. How many times have you received relationship advice from someone in the middle of a divorce, financial advice from someone who has declared bankruptcy more than once, or educational advice from someone who doesn't use their degree or never even went to college?

If someone hasn't been there before you, they are not qualified to give you that advice. Sometimes, people email me asking for marriage advice, and I respond with one question: how long have you been married? If you've been married longer than me, I cannot give you any advice because I haven't been married that long. I don't know what it feels like.

I've been working for myself since February 2010. The day I was fired, and the boats were burned behind me, I had a choice to make. I could build my own business, or I could curl up on the floor and cry. Believe me, curling up was tempting. But I decided to embrace my destiny instead, and I am here today to show you how I succeeded and help you do the same.

My name is Jonathan Green. Today, I am thirty-seven years old. I have three children. Just last week, my third child was born, but he is with us today for one reason and one reason only: because I always have a plan C.

Last year, my wife and I lost a child to a miscarriage. We fought harder than you could ever imagine for that child, but it wasn't enough. This year, on the morning of my son's birth, a doctor told us that she had to run a final test. If it failed, she would have to terminate the pregnancy. The doctor spoke fast enough that my wife didn't understand what she meant as English is her third language and we rarely use the word terminate around the house.

We walked out of the office and as my wife prepared for the heartbeat test for our son, who otherwise was in perfect condition, she noticed me texting my father. While I tried to hold it together perfectly, she realized something was wrong. She asked me what that word meant, and I had no choice but to tell her the truth.

Her eyes filled with tears and rage.

If we were in anything less than our current economic situation, my son would not have made it that day. The hospital had allowed us to prepay for a birth package. We had everything in place. We had gone through all the tests. We had done everything. We could have walked out with no bill that day if we had let them deliver our child after he passed that test.

But I have a rule. If someone threatens to kill my child, I don't let them deliver my child into the world. We called our private backup doctor, who is quite expensive. Later that day, after my wife was induced, my son went into distress. Every time my wife had a contraction, his heartbeat would slow down.

Things were getting worse. The umbilical cord was wrapped around his neck, and I was called down to the emergency room and told that we would have to perform an emergency Cesarean. Upon hearing those words, my wife did something unbelievable. She screamed, "I don't think so!" and immediately delivered our son.

I can tell you without a single bit of doubt that if we hadn't been able to afford the private doctor, my son would not be here today. When I tell you what I believe about setting up other financial plans and strategies, I don't speak to you from a high ivory tower. I speak to you from a place in the dirt – a place of survival.

I don't want you to go through these terrible situations. The birth of my child ended up costing thirteen times more than what we prepaid to the hospital. And they didn't even give us a credit for our prepayment. They punished us for going with a private doctor.

When your family is on the line, and everything's at stake, you have to be able to do what it takes to protect them. After losing my job during a blizzard and hitting rock bottom, I had no choice but to strive for the top. Since then, I've written more than two hundred books for myself and for clients. As I built my business and my reputation, I created direct response products that have generated over $10,000,000 in sales.

The day after paying that massive hospital bill, I signed a long-term lease on the hotel I bought for my wife. She has her own business too, now. See, just like I know health insurance doesn't pay out, life insurance likes to play games too. I discovered that I could buy my wife a self-sustaining business for far less than most of us pay in life insurance premiums. I no longer have to worry that my children will be protected if something happens to me because the business supports itself with enough left over to take care of my family forever.

All these things have come into place because I believe in leveraging who you are, what you can do, what you know, and who you know, and I learned how to generate massive revenue on the Internet.

I live on a tropical island. In two days, I'll be moving into that hotel we just took over. No, I'm not going to tell you exactly where it is, but I will tell you it's somewhere awesome. If you join my Facebook group and follow my blog, you'll see pictures and videos of me walking along the beach in front of palm trees all the time.

If the thought of running your own business, generating revenue online, being in charge of your own financial destiny, or living on a tropical island does not interest you, please stop reading this book. Do not follow the advice of someone whose life you don't want to emulate!

But if the idea of having total control of your life – of being in a situation where your boss can fire you, and you can walk out and just say "Okay!" without your lifestyle changing – if that appeals to you, then you're going to love this book because that's what I want to create for you.

One of my friends was an Executive Vice President at one of the largest companies in the world. I can guarantee you've seen one of their vans in the last twenty-four hours.

He got swept in one of their downsizings, and he went from making six figures a year to nothing – from a five-bedroom mansion with a Hummer and the top-of-the-line Lexus to living in a studio apartment with a mold problem. It can happen to anyone, but if you stay on this journey with me, it will not happen to you.

# 3

# WHAT YOU WILL ACCOMPLISH, AKA UNLEASH THE BEAST

W estern education is designed to turn thinkers into drones. Creativity is squashed, individual thought is minimized, and questioning is not allowed. Think about what happens when you first go to school, and you're full of imagination and wonder. You're passionate about the arts, and everything seems possible. But as you get older, the rules become stricter, and you're told, "Do this." "Don't do that."

The main thing you learn at college is how to turn papers in on time. In fact, that's basically the only useful skill 99 percent of college graduates walk away with. There's only one thermometer I personally measure education with, including what I teach you:

Do you make more money with that knowledge than it cost you to acquire it?

If you read this book, and after everything I teach you, you don't make the cost of the book back, then you are entitled to leave me a bad review. I'm willing to stand up to that.

Most tertiary education institutions aren't. Walk into any law school admissions office in the United States and ask,

"What percentage of your graduates from last year are currently employed?" They'll give you a very impressive figure – 80 or even 90 percent.[1] But if you ask them how many of those people are employed as lawyers, they'll throw you out of the office. (Do it at an undergraduate university, and they'll bury you in an unmarked grave.)[2]

That's a coveted, secret piece of information. If they revealed it, no one would ever go to law school again. Before you think I've got something against law schools, you should know that most of my family besides me are lawyers. I almost went to law school myself.

Universities do the same thing. They make you promises when you enroll, "We'll get you a sweet job." "Everyone who graduates here is employed."

Have you ever noticed that all the tour guides at every single university were students there first? They couldn't get a real job after graduating, so they stayed where they felt safe, and now they're leading eighteen-year-old newbies straight to the slaughter. These young minds will enter the world in massive amounts of debt,[3] and the only thing they will learn is how to be an employee.

### Trusting in the Machine

We grew up as a generation under the promise of social security. Every year, the ratio between workers and those relying on social security to survive gets worse. Soon there won't be enough people to support all of us entering retirement. Do you have a plan for social security collapsing? What is your plan B?

The last thing you want is to get hit with a financial shock when you're too old to re-enter the market. Do you really want to spend eight hours a day at the front of a big box retailer, welcoming new customers, while a manager fifty years younger than you shouts at you every time your smile slips?

The government, larger corporations, and even certain insurance funds all make the same promise – when you get too old to work, they will take care of you. But what happens when you live too long? Most retirement plans assume you'll only last a few years after you retire. But some people retire in their sixties and live past one hundred. Do you think your retirement fund has a plan to support you for ten times longer than their initial strategy?

There is a reckoning coming, and those of us entering retirement are going to be the ones crushed when the entire building collapses.

Everyone out there is promising to take care of you, but they are all liars.

## Become the Master

This book is the opposite. I'm going to teach you how to be the master of your own destiny. By the time you finish reading this book, you will find the asset you should leverage first. There's nothing more important to me than you achieving that success.

The beauty is that there are many ways for you to accomplish that. Rather than this book teaching you a single system – how to blog, how to sell books, or how to start an eBay store – we're going to put together a strategy that will allow you to find what you're best at and turn that into money *fast*. That's the measure of success.

If the majority of people graduating from college were working jobs other than baristas, I wouldn't complain about the higher education institution. When I graduated from my university and asked for help finding a job, they gave me the link to a job forum. They sent me to the early Internet days version of monster.com. I discovered that if I got a job at a fast food joint, they would tell those poor eighteen-year-old newbies that one more graduate had a job.

We're going to find something in your heart of hearts, and we're going to use it to build a business, unlock your destiny and put you in a situation where you're financially secure.

In this book, you will learn the five elemental forces that hold most people back from achieving entrepreneurial freedom. You will learn how to break through those barriers and discover just what's possible on the other side of freedom. Together, we are going to find the best asset, whether it is a skill, possession, or contact, and leverage that to create fast revenue. The sooner you make that first dollar after reading this book, the more likely you are to stay the course and make it all the way to the top of the mountain.

Once you have made enough money to say goodbye to the job you hate (unless you love it), we will begin working on passive revenue systems. Believe me, there is nothing more magical than waking up to more money in your bank account than when you went to sleep.

You don't have to quit your job. If you love what you're doing, keep doing it. This is about providing a second layer of security so that if something happens to that job, your family is not in dire straits. They're protected, your children are protected, your loved ones are safe, and you can continue having a nice life.

## 4

## WHAT DO YOU WANT FROM LIFE?

This is a book about *doing*, not just reading. I've already carried the weight for three whole chapters; it's time for us to start working together. This isn't a motivational book. I don't want you to feel good after reading it. I don't want you to feel pumped or excited. I want you to feel money in your hand. I want you to have tangible results.

In order to maximize the odds of that happening, I need you to be active. Do not read this entire book without participating in the activities. I've already shared with you some of the most personal and painful stories of my life not to show that I'm tough, but in the hopes that if I go first, you'll go second.

Take a moment right now and get a notebook. If you have to drive to the pharmacy to buy one, do it now. On the front, write your first name in big letters followed by "Breakthrough Journal." In this Journal, you're going to write down your answers to every activity. You're going to draw pictures and mind maps in there. Together, we're going to create a vision in that Journal.

On the first page, you're going to answer your very first question: "What do I want?" I encourage you to be as specific as possible. In my first bestseller *Serve No Master*, I encourage people to write down the answer to three mathematical questions:

1. How much money do you need to make to stop going into debt?

2. How much money beyond that do you need to make to quit your job?

3. How much money do you need to make to live your dream lifestyle?

As my writing has matured, so has my audience. More and more of my followers are now looking at a new set of three questions.

1. How much money do you need to supplement social security when you retire?

2. How much money do you need to maintain your current standard of living when you retire?

3. How much money do you need to enjoy retirement?

We're going to build on this exercise when you describe your perfect life in your Journal:

- Where do you live?
- Do you have kids? How many?
- How much money comes in every day?
- How much time do you spend working?
- What do you spend your day doing?

I listened to an interview with a screenwriter once, who was talking about how many people ask him: "How do you know when it's time to quit?" He said something pretty brilliant: "If you fantasize about being a screenwriter, you have a problem, and you should probably quit. However, if your dream is to write screenplays, then you're in the right business."[1]

I like writing books more than I like telling people that I'm a writer. I'm *passionate* about writing. Find what you love and what you want to spend your time doing. To find out what you're passionate about, ask yourself: "If I never needed money again, what would I spend all day doing?"

Write down your answer in your journal.

I hope you see now that the questions in this book aren't rhetorical. If a sentence ends in a question mark, you should write down your answer in your Journal.

I'm one of the most prolific writers in the world, and what I wish I could do is write more books. That's how you know you're doing what you love. The only other thing I wish I could do more is spending time with my children. Fortunately, the majority of the time I spend writing, I can see them playing. I like to dictate on the beach and watch them play in the sand. It brings great joy into my life.

Take a moment now to describe your perfect life in your Journal. Even better, draw a mind map or a picture. We are going to materialize your destination by creating the answer to a mathematical formula.

If this book works, then whatever you write in your Journal will be what happens.

If you draw a picture of you on a yacht drinking a Piña Colada, then your proof statement becomes: "If *Breakthrough* works, then I will be on a yacht sipping a Piña Colada."

I don't begrudge your desire to be wealthy or even super wealthy. My best friend from college once said to me, "Money can't buy happiness, but it can buy air conditioning, a front yard, vacations, and a good education for your kids." That stuck with me because there's a lot you can do that makes it easier to be happy when we remove financial stress from your life.

Spend some time creating your vision. If you're already stuck here, you can email me and ask for help. Every single week, I get five to ten emails that start with, "I'm not sure if you're going to reply to this," or, "I wonder if you'll see this." I always do.

I reply to every single one.

If somehow you email me and don't hear back, send another one two days later because it means I didn't see it. I don't have a virtual assistant, a secretary, or someone else to check my email. I always reply personally.

If you're stuck here, and you're not sure what you want from life, reach out. Even better, you can join my Facebook group, where loads of people who are already achieving success will share their stories with you. There's always someone ready to spend time with you and help you out.

When you have a firm answer for what you want from life, and you've written it down in your Breakthrough Journal, let's get right to the next chapter.

## 5

## BLEED WITH ME, AND I'LL BLEED WITH YOU

The journey we're about to embark upon is going to be amazing, but there are parts of it that will be scary. You're going to have moments of self-doubt where you might think, "I'm not good enough." "I'm not smart enough." "I'm afraid of rejection."

This book is built around helping you break through every one of those fears, but you're going to have moments of doubt, and that's okay. Rather than pretending it won't happen or that it doesn't happen to me, I want to be honest with you.

It's hard to do this on your own. Some members of my Facebook group shared with me that they've been doing their best online for eight years, but they only found success when they joined the group because they had other people to talk to. They finally found someone who could answer their questions and show them what they were doing right and wrong.

It's often a small change that can revolutionize someone's life, and that's why it's so important that you realize this is not like other books. This is a cooperative venture.

We're on this journey together. Even though I'm speaking first in every chapter of this book, you can reply to me, and we can start a dialogue. As long as you're willing to try the exercises and go through the process, I will stay on this journey with you. I will continue to answer your questions. I'll continue to post videos, offer live training sessions, interact with you and guide you.

My commitment to you is that I will never be the first one to quit. You might stumble ten times, but every time you look up, I'm still reaching down with my hand to say, "We can still do this. We're getting closer."

You never have to be alone again.

I believe in what I do, and there's a reason I have decided keep it a niche rather than operating in a bigger market, even though I could sell much more. There's a reason you picked up this book. We were meant to go on this journey together. Stick with me until the end of the book.

Let me have a chance to revolutionize your way of thinking and show you what's possible. I promise that if you give me that much, I'll give you so much more. I'm passionate about my following, and I'm dedicated to spending time with them. If you stay on this journey with me, I will stay on this journey with you. If you're willing to bleed with me, I am willing to bleed with you.

# 6

## FIVE RINGS TO RULE THEM ALL

You are probably familiar with the book *The Art of War*. There are a lot of Sun Tzu fans (and people who've never read the book) out there who quote it all the time. I grew up at a time when karate was for nerds, and having read *The Art of War* made me the exception instead of the cool kid.

I have a desire to stay a little bit counterculture, one step ahead of everyone else. We've all heard stories about *The Art of War*. We've seen it applied to business and to everything else. That resource has been pretty well mined.

There's a different book that I prefer. It's not quite so ancient. It's Japanese instead of Chinese, but it's brilliant. It's *The Book of Five Rings* by Miyamoto Musashi. He was a Japanese samurai whose story has been a little bit embellished over the years through fictionalized books and movies. The end of his life is questionable, since he apparently disappeared into the mists one day, as mythical figures often do.

He was known for a few things. The first was that he never lost a battle. He was a sword fighter who dueled masters of many different martial arts and never lost once. According to his book, he was also the first to draw a second sword and use it against an enemy. He was the first person to pull out the wakizashi in his left hand, the Japanese short sword that was traditionally used only for suicide, so he could fight multiple opponents at once.

He was such a great fighter that he eventually stopped using metal swords. He carved two oars into wooden sticks and began to fight with those because winning was too easy for him. He was so good at his art form that he needed to give his opponents an advantage. Unlike giving your boss a few strokes on the golf course, his life was on the line.

*The Book of Five Rings* is brilliant because it teaches fighting through his belief in five elements which he calls rings: wind, ground, water, fire, and void. In this book, we're going to go through the five elements you need to dominate in order to unlock your greatest potential:

**Element One WIND – Mindset.**

We often think of the wind as the least important or powerful of the elemental forces, but that couldn't be further from the truth. We can survive three weeks without food, three days without water, but only three minutes without air. In the Ring of Wind, you will learn how to master the mindset of success and break through distraction to begin your new entrepreneurial journey.

So often, it's the little distractions that knock us off-track and keep us from achieving our destinies. As you master the Ring of Wind, you will become someone who is not distracted by passing thoughts and irrelevant distractions. You will become the master of your thoughts. Your desires and your actions will move into alignment with each other.

**Element Two EARTH – Barriers.**

Earth is strong and powerful. It is the very ground we walk on. When we think of the ultimate barrier, it is a stone wall, and the ultimate obstacle is a mountain. There is nothing more challenging than to climb and cross over a mountain made of earth's mighty stone.

There is a barrier right now standing between you and the life you deserve. That barrier feels thick and strong, and you may very well feel powerless to overcome it.

In the Ring of Earth, you will learn to claim mastery over your barriers. You will learn to shatter the walls that have held you back from the life you deserve for far too long. As you shatter that mountain, you will look back and say, "It seemed taller from the other side." We will smash those mountains into molehills.

**Element Three WATER – Assets.**

Water is so much more than something to drink when you are thirsty. While it's most commonly found in liquid form, when it's solid or gaseous, water is terrifying. A large ice cube sank the largest passenger cruise ship in history. If you think water vapor is a joke, see what happens when you get a faceful of steam.

Right now you have an incredible amount of power inside you trapped as unrealized potential. In the Ring of Water, we are going to convert your assets into powerful ice and your skills into dreadful steam. We will assess your true value and begin to build a plan to get you paid what you are actually worth, rather than what your boss thinks you'll take.

**Element Four FLAME – Fast Money.**

Fire is an exciting and terrifying force. The scariest part of fire is not the heat; it's the speed. Fire moves very fast, and it's time for you to experience fast results.

In the Ring of Flame, we are going to set fire to your current salary and set realistic financial goals. You are going to make real money here, and it's going to shock you. With the speed of fire, you will leverage your assets into a new revenue stream. Very simply, I want you to put real money in your pocket *fast*. We are going to find the shortest path between you and new revenue, outside of your current 9-5.


**Element Five VOID – Business Models.**

The void is a place of great emptiness. It's a place where nothing exists yet. And that is what makes it so powerful. In outer space, we are separated from the other four Rings, and we cannot survive. The power of Void is its potential. Here you can create or accomplish anything. You can truly become that which you have always dreamed of – limitless.

We will forge a path to your greatness – a place where you can achieve the ultimate goal of *Breakthrough* – to make money while you sleep. Passive income can be found in the Ring of Void. That silence and emptiness of void are waiting for you to fill them with your vision for greatness.


**Unite the Five Elements**

In the Ring of Flame, you will build a new revenue stream that pays for time. With enough time to work on your real project, it's time to spread your wings and build passive and long-lasting revenue streams online. Get paid with fast money to learn the very skills you will use to build your online business. Bring the five elements together to build a complete business. With the right mindset and freedom from your previous barriers, business models you would have thought impossible in the past suddenly become achievable. Now you have the skills, knowledge, and financial runway to develop them. Get ready to take flight.

Your approach to each of these elements should be the approach of mastery. Focus on one and master it before you move onto the next one. Unlike traditional martial arts, it won't take you eighty years or a lifetime to master these elements. Each of them should be very quick because only a small percentage of each Ring will apply to you individually.

Some of the issues and challenges we're going to cover won't apply to you. We're going to find the one that is relevant to you, overcome it, and move on to the next challenge until you are ready to achieve your breakthrough.

I call each lesson a Ring because rings are circular. There is no perfect order in which to learn these lessons. You are more than welcome to read the Rings in any order that you like. Many people find that reading this book a second time reveals more insight as they have context from the following Rings.

However you decide to consume this book, make sure that you complete all five Rings.

# 7

# INTRODUCTION REFLECTION QUESTIONS

1. Do you have debt in your life right now?
2. Have you ever tracked your finances to see how much money you've spent on paying debt and interest fees since you turned eighteen?
3. How would you feel if you could get all that money back right now?
4. Does the idea of financial freedom and the ability to endure a financial shock resonate with you?
5. If you lost your job tomorrow, how much runway would you have before your family was in trouble?
6. Do you feel like high education has the same value it did ten, twenty, or fifty years ago?
7. Do you now have a clear vision of what you want to achieve from this book?
8. Have you tried to start projects in the past that failed because you had no one to share ideas with or support you when things got tough?

9. Does the idea of working on the five elements of a successful business as part of a cohesive system resonate with you?

10. Are you excited to dig into the first element?

## INTRODUCTION ACTION

I deally, you've already completed this action step, but I know some people get so excited with reading that they don't want to put the book down for any reason. If you haven't started your Breakthrough Journal yet, now is a *great* time to start.

You have reached a natural stopping point in the book, and if you don't start taking notes now, you're going to regret it. Pull out an old notebook, turn it upside down and start writing from the back if you have to.

Before you move on to the next section, I encourage you to go back through this section and write down all your answers to the reflection questions. These answers will be the foundation for the following sections.

# ADDITIONAL INFORMATION

In my books, I often reference a book I like or a software tool I use. Rather than filling this book with links you'll never remember, I have put all of that additional information in a single place. To find more information on the tool, people, and websites I talk about, you can visit my special page:

ServeNoMaster.com/Breakthrough

That's the only link you have to remember. Much easier for you to remember, since it's the name of this book, and much easier for my editor, who doesn't have to constantly update the links as I change my favorite software tools.

# ELEMENT ONE WIND – MINDSET OF SUCCESS

# 10

## A BREATH OF AIR

A ir is a powerful force. In our world of spaceships and hermetically sealed buildings, we forget how much power the wind truly has. Every year, we see major hurricanes leveling cities. It's not the rain you have to worry about; it's the power of wind tearing cities apart.

Wind starts as a whisper. It's a little thought that plants itself in the back of your head. That little voice that tells you that you're not smart enough, you're not good enough, or it's too late.

Wind is powerful but also invisible. We can't see it – we can only see how it affects a hat flying off a bald man's head or a flag whipping under a strong breeze. In the same way, you can't look at an emotion sitting at a table. You can't draw a picture of a thought. You can only see the effects of your thoughts and emotions on the world around you.

Just because you can't see something, it does not mean it's not powerful.

The longer a bad thought has been living in your mind, the more powerful it has become. Over time, we forget the course of our false beliefs and invisible barriers – we just take them to be true. For many of you, this Ring is going to be very painful. We are going to look many of your false beliefs directly in the eye, and when you realize that you've been limited by a false belief for decades, it is very painful. Our natural reaction to a painful truth is to reject it rather than to admit we have been making poor decisions for so long.

I ask you to bear with me in this section. We will do our best to rip the scales from your eyes slowly, but it's going to require that you stay the course.

While the wind can be a destructive force, we can learn to harness it with sails, giving us enough power to sail across the ocean. Ships can use wind to go directly against the wind. That's how powerful our ingenuity truly is. It's time to replace faith in false assumptions with faith in yourself.

Prepare to spread your wings and harness the Ring of Wind.

# 11

# FOCUS

Achieving mastery or success in any area of life requires great focus. We live our lives surrounded by too many distractions. If you don't put a plan in place to resist those distractions, you'll feel like you're busy but never accomplish anything. The second you sit down at your desk, open your email and activate your chat accounts, you'll start to receive a barrage of messages about small, meaningless issues that you "need" to deal with throughout the day.

When you're working for someone else, your only goal is to fill each day. Despite feeling dreadful when I lost my job, I was already spinning my wheels. I was not trained for bureaucracy, and when I was thrust into a position where 99 percent of my job was to pretend I was working, I didn't know what to do. I was flustered and confused.

The first task my boss gave me was supposed to take six months. She said, "Focus on this every day for the next six months, and you should be ready around summertime." Three hours later, the task was completed under budget and beyond her wildest expectations. Suddenly, we had a problem.

Bureaucrats hate initiative. My working fast didn't impress her. Instead, it made it look like she was moving slowly. She saw my success as a critique of her inability to complete tasks in a timely fashion. She was already starting to regret her decision to hire me, but she decided to give me another shot with a task that she knew would take me far longer.

She gave me a task which was supposed to take an entire year to bring across the finish line. I was finished the next day, and my fate was sealed. She began looking for a reason to terminate me before anyone above her could ask the most dreaded of questions, "If it only took him a day, why did you say it would take a year?"

The larger the organization is, the more people inside of it are expected to spin their wheels. If you work too hard and make too many waves, the other people who are just coasting through will do everything they can to get rid of you. If you're not sure what I'm talking about, head over the DMV and see what it's like to get a driver's license.

When in doubt, people default to a state of passivity. They focus on filling their days, not on the quality of what they accomplish. For entrepreneurs, this problem begins with a lack of focus. That's why the very first task was for you to visualize and draw a picture of the center of your bullseye. When you know the target you're aiming towards, you can measure whether or not you're moving closer to that goal.

At the end of every day, you must ask yourself a very simple question:

Have I moved closer towards that goal or further away
from it?

This binary question allows you to assess the quality of
your efforts that day. It's easy to be distracted. We have
family, obligations, and social rules. Many of our goals are
so far away we can't really see them.

The reason so many of us are ill-prepared for retirement
is that it seems so far away. Yesterday, I turned thirty-eight. I
have a friend who joined the military at eighteen, and that
means he just hit his twenty-year mark. He can retire from
active duty now. Something that seemed so far away came at
me like a freight train. Time moves faster than we think, and
yet retirement seems ages away.

Only when we enter our sixties do we start to think
about the future and suddenly realize we won't be retiring
anytime soon. Not because we love working, but because we
have no choice. Our chickens have come home to roost.

It's time to put a clear and focused goal in front of you –
something that can drive your action.

As we master this first element, we are going to create
goals that are actionable and effective so that they work well
enough to motivate you. A goal is effective if it is enough to
change your action. If you have a goal that's ten years away
but you still move towards it every single day, then that goal
is good enough. However, for some people, the goal has to
be just one day or just a month away.

## Reflection Questions

1. Do you feel closer to your goal than you did
   yesterday?

2. What is your primary cause of distraction throughout your day?
3. Have you planned for the future or spent so much time focusing on today that the future was forgotten?
4. What could you accomplish with nothing to distract you?

**Take Action**

Design a distraction-free zone. Create a time and place where you will focus on the ideas, lessons, and projects that arise from this book. It can be a special room in your house or a special set of headphones that you wear to let your family know you are not to be disturbed.

I work from home, and creating a focus zone is critical to my productivity. With three little kids running around, there is always some emergency desperate to distract me. You might need to wait until the kids go to bed or turn the upstairs bathroom into your sanctuary.

Find a place where you can work and get things done. Perhaps a place without Internet access.

# 12

# REAL GOALS

I have covered goal setting extensively in other books, and loads of other authors have covered this ground before, so I am going to keep it straightforward. There are four simple ways to tell if a goal is any good.

**1. A goal must have a "pass or fail" element.**

Can you tell whether or not you succeeded with the goal? If there's no way to say whether you succeeded or failed, it's not a goal; it's an opinion. "I'd like to lose some weight." "I'd like to make some more money." Although these are nice things to say, they're meaningless. They won't change your life. Everyone says them every single New Year's Eve.

The critical element is: can it be measured with a "yes or no?" Instead of, "I want to lose some weight," how about, "I want to lose five pounds." Now you can measure if you accomplished the goal: did you lose five pounds or not?

## 2. A goal must have a due date.

If you say, "I want to lose five pounds," but there's no end date, you can still be working on it fifty years from now. A goal is not very effective without a deadline.

If you have a clear due date, you will push yourself towards it. In school, many students wait until the last minute to work on a project. Between one night and one week before the project is due, they switch into "deadline mode." For some people, it's the night before.

How effective would you be if your professor gave you three days to work on that project instead of thirty? You would turn in something just as good without spending twenty-seven days procrastinating. And how efficient would you be if you had a new deadline every three days? You could accomplish ten times as much in the same amount of time!

Due dates increase our effectiveness and force us to be efficient. I'm currently working with a consultant who is mostly a mathematician and analyst. He looks at my numbers, puts them into spreadsheets and tells me where to focus on improving my website. It's all math, which is very unnatural to me. I had to bring someone from the outside to give it an objective viewpoint.

Every time he tells me I should change something, I put a hard deadline on it, so I make fast change. When you have a short deadline, you do the minimum necessary to pass that goal point. Some of the pages I built for my website aren't perfect, but they're good enough to get me to the next point. Deadlines force you to stay on track and allow you to see whether or not you hit that goal.

### 3. Your goals must be public.

At the very least, write down your goals. I have some good news! You've already started your Breakthrough Journal, which is a great place to write down your goals. At least it's in the real world.

If you just keep your goal in your mind, it won't be reliable. We all have a bit of a revisionist history in our minds, don't we? We remember things differently than other people. This is why eyewitness testimony is notoriously unreliable.[1] Ten people can watch the same crime and pick ten different suspects from the lineup.

When you take a goal out of your mind and write it down, it becomes real. Now you can't go, "What was my goal again? Was I going to lose five pounds? No, I think I said three. Oh look, I lost four! I beat my goal." I don't want you to lie to yourself.

The more public you make it, the more powerful that goal becomes. When you post, "I'm going to lose thirty pounds in thirty days," as your Facebook status, it gets real. The next day you can write, "Twenty-nine pounds and twenty-nine days to go," and everyone can see it. Knowing that everyone's watching will increase the effectiveness of your goal setting and will make you more likely to achieve the mindset of success.

### 4. A good goal must be divisible.

You should be able to break it apart into smaller components and tasks you can perform over time on the way to that goal.

I'm part of a lot of writers' groups. I love surrounding

myself online with people who write in different ways. There are many ways to motivate yourself, and watching other people self-motivate keeps me excited. Someone who just finished their first book recently posted the news on one of my groups, and their success got me even more motivated.

The process of writing a book is beautiful because it's so divisible. Most people say, "I want to write a book." That's a "yes or no," but if you say, "I want to write a 45,000-word book in the next nine months," now we know how many words you need to write every single day to hit your goal. You can track your progress daily.

You need to write 5,000 words a month to stay on pace. Divide that by how many words you need per day, and you can really track yourself. This is how we set a goal and turn it into a journey.

Success doesn't come from big goals. It comes from daily repetition and consistency. Success comes from having a goal that says, "This is what I have to accomplish today," every single day. That's how you set effective goals. As Greg S. Reid wrote,

*A DREAM WRITTEN down with a date becomes a goal. A goal broken down into steps becomes a plan. A plan backed by action makes your dreams come true.*

## Reflection Questions

1. Have you set goals incorrectly in the past without realizing it?

2. Can you see why so many New Year's resolutions fail?

3. Did you notice that the very first task in this book was to write down specific financial numbers for your goals?

4. Can you strengthen those goals by attaching target dates to them? Why don't you do that right now?

5. Can you see how daisy-chaining together a series of small goals can keep you in a perpetual state of "deadline mode?"

6. How focused are you when you are in deadline mode?

7. Can you see how the seeds planted earlier in this book are already starting to grow into something powerful?

8. How much would you accomplish in life if you achieved every single goal you envisioned?

## Take Action

Your first activity is to set a real goal with a real timeline. We started the book with three financial goals. The first one was how much money you need to make to stop increasing your debt. You might have already passed that first goal and be on the path to quitting your job. That's fine. Just use the number from the second goal.

Take your financial goal and turn it into a real goal. Give it a timeline and put it somewhere public. With a big sign above the bathroom sink that says: "Make $6,000 by June 14 and quit your job," the odds of that goal happening go through the roof.

Here are some other possible goals:

1. Pay off my biggest credit card debt in six months.
2. Pay off my mortgage within the next five years.
3. Raise $10,000 for my retirement fund in ninety days.

Follow the steps from this lesson and turn your first goal from imaginary into concrete.

# 13

## ACCOUNTABILITY

L et me ask you a question. It might be a tough one to hear, but it's an important one for you to answer before we start to dial down into where account-ability lies.

Who do you bend your knee to? What master do you serve?[1]

We all serve someone. For many of us, it's the boss who doesn't appreciate our work, steals credit for our efforts, and makes us work overtime. I'm constantly baffled by the postgraduate world. You spend years putting in massive amounts of unpaid work. You might even discover or invent something amazing and get no financial recompense.

To achieve true freedom of mindset, you have to under-stand where you're coming from.

Do you feel a sense of obligation to a person or orga-nization?

Here's a way to test this. When you started reading this book, and I started talking about setting up additional revenue streams and not trusting your boss, did you feel guilty? Did you feel like I was telling you that you should betray your employer?

If the answer is yes, that means you feel a sense of loyalty toward them, and that's no crime. The real crime is that they feel no loyalty toward you. It's one of the great tragedies of our culture. You've got to look out for yourself. If you feel any sense of guilt about the idea of setting up a backup business in case you lose your job, you serve someone dramatically.

Many of us bend our knee to a job that we can't wait to escape. That's awesome – at least you've begun to free your mind. That's where this journey begins. If you don't free your mind, you'll never free your body.

I'm not driven by a master above me anymore. Instead, I'm driven by those who depend on me. Why do I work every day? Why do I work so hard? Why am I constantly writing books beyond it being my passion? I have an obligation to my children; they depend on me.

Look around you and see who depends on you. Think about how that affects your life and how it drives you.

When I started to have children, everything changed. When it was just my wife and me, we could live fast and loose. We could live on ramen if we have to. With no obligations, we would easily decide to take six months off and chill on the beach. You can move to a new country to "find yourself" when nobody is relying on you.

But once you start having kids, you think about things you never thought about before. You think about getting three different health insurance accounts. You think about education, stability, and what happens if you die. It's a great sense of obligation. I want to protect my children and prepare them to enter the world when they're ready to start their own businesses.

You may have already done your best for your children and as you look to the future, how does the thought of leaving a legacy to them sound? Would it be amazing to have a fully-funded retirement and still have something left to leave to the kids...even if you live longer than the Social Security Agency every imagined?

That's why accountability is so important. It goes beyond just thinking about who you're loyal to and who depends on you. You need a group of people around you at your level to provide you with a sense of accountability, to tell you whether or not you've done a good job, to check if you got distracted or lost focus and to call you out when you make mistakes.

I've been a part of different masterminds for most of my online career. I meet once a week with other people who are at the same business level as me, so we can talk about our frustrations, challenges, and successes. It helps us stay in alignment with our goals and maintain our mindsets.

Whether serving a master or working for yourself, there are going to be bad days, and there are going to be challenges. We want to put a system in place to protect ourselves from them. Surrounding yourself with other people is how you become more powerful. As iron sharpens iron, one person sharpens another.

It's very dangerous to be caught up in your own mind and not speak to other people. If you get locked in a prison cell in isolation, and you're not allowed to talk to other people, it doesn't take very long for insanity to set in.[2] Even monkeys go insane when isolated.[3] That's why I encourage you to find other people to mastermind and communicate with who are on the same journey as you. They will hold you accountable for your goals and tasks and help you to stay the course.

We are the average of the five people we spend most of our time with. If you spend all of your time with five fat people, you'll become fat. If you spend your time with five people who just play video games, you'll get good at video games. If you spend your time with five millionaires, you'll become a millionaire.

Surround yourself with people who are a bit further up the mountain and are continuing to grow. I don't want to be around people who are frozen and stuck at the same income level for five years. I want to keep moving and growing.

There are many ways you can create accountability in your life. Writing a goal in your Journal is the beginning. Writing down goals and the answers to each Reflection Question in this book will make you accountable to yourself.

Go beyond that. Post that goal in my Facebook group. Now other people can hold you to it.

Write your goals and dreams on a big piece of poster board and tack it to the wall so that it's the first thing you see every morning and the last thing you see every night. It will be a constant reminder.

My friend Jim got a big piece of poster board and wrote the amount of money he wanted to make when he was struggling to make ends meet, living in a shared apartment in London. It was a big number, and the first time I saw it, I thought it was ridiculous. Three years later, he hit that number. There's no better way to shut up a naysayer than to crush that goal.

Before you go any further, your task is to tell at least one other person about your goal. The more public, the better. You don't have to get a tattoo, but I'm okay with you printing it on a T-shirt. The louder you say it, the more likely you are to achieve it.

## Reflection Questions

1. Do you feel a sense of loyalty to a person or institution who does not respond with the same loyalty?
2. Have you been let down by them in the past?
3. Does the thought of making your goal public make you nervous?
4. Are you surrounded by people who lift you up or hold you back from your dreams?
5. Do you need a new support group to help you grow?
6. What is your ideal supportive situation?

## Take Action

Find a group of five people who are on the same path as you. People with the same entrepreneurial spirit and the drive to change their destinies. You can find them in your current social group, online, and even within my Facebook group. Commit to meeting once a week to discuss what you are working on and bounce ideas off each other.

If your group is online, try to meet for a video call. Video calls are far more affecting than voice-only calls at accountability. Commit to making your group a priority, and your success will accelerate.

# 14

## BUSINESS IS NOT A HOBBY

We treat money very differently depending on our emotional state or mindset. When you're on vacation, you'll pay a price for a drink or a hamburger that you would never pay when you're not on vacation. Hotels and resorts obviously take advantage of this. They know you'll say to yourself, "I'm on vacation, I'm going to splurge," and they raise their prices accordingly.

When we invest money, we want to make it back. But when we spend money on entertainment, it's gone forever.

If you think of your business as a hobby, you will never succeed.

Nobody ever succeeds at turning a hobby into a real business until they change their mindset. Do not treat this book as a hobby manual. It's only when you treat something like a real business that success becomes a possibility. You must alter your perspective immediately.

Writing is not my hobby. My website is not my hobby.

Recording videos, building courses, and supporting my family is not my hobby; it's my business. I have a bookkeeper who tracks every single penny I spend and knows exactly where it goes. When I waste it, she points that out.

You need to keep accurate records and know your numbers. I learned my lesson last year. My bookkeeper had a tragedy and disappeared for six months. When I hired a new bookkeeper, I realized all of my previous bookkeeper's records were stored remotely on her computer.

Needless to say, I don't do that anymore. Now everything is digitally stored on a different platform that I can access anytime I want. You can never rely on someone else. Sometimes, things outside of your control happen, and you need to protect yourself from that.

Before you spend a huge amount of money on accounting software, start small and just keep a physical book. My wife keeps a notebook of every penny she spends because we used to fight about money, as most couples do. I would say, "Where did all the money go?" When we first started dating, she often had no answer, but now, every time I ask that question, she pulls out her notebook and gives me a list of everything she bought and where the money went. I have learned it's usually me that blew through our spending money.

I no longer ask my wife to pull out that notebook because every time she does, I'm at fault. That's how powerful keeping your financial records can be. You have to decide if you're going to be a hero or a zero from the beginning. The way you start is the way you'll finish.

If you're having a bit of fun, and this seems kind of interesting but, "Hey, I'm going to wait until I make money to start keeping records." Guess what? You'll never do it. When you finally do try and switch over, you're going to have big problems.

Before I had a bookkeeper or an accountant, I followed the same mindset. The problem is that my first year in business, I replaced my income from the job I lost. And the second year, I made twenty times more money. I experienced exponential growth, but I had terrible records, and the first accountant I tried to hire didn't really appreciate that.

She asked me, "How much money do you make?"

I replied, "I don't know."

"What do you do when you run out of money?"

"Well, I go make more."

She didn't throw me out of her office, but it was a pretty uncomfortable silence. Needless to say, we decided not to work together.

Making money is a skill that you're going to master when you follow the principles in this book and break through. When that happens, you're going to really want those records, so your accountant doesn't have an aneurysm. If you don't treat money with respect, money will not treat you with respect. If you don't track where your money goes, there's a very high chance you will fail.

Every month, I spend a lot of money on advertising. I have to be extremely fastidious with my record keeping. Just a change in 2 or 3 percentage points in one of my advertising campaigns is the difference between making money and losing money. If I incorrectly estimate and believe that a campaign is profitable, I will start to increase my budget tenfold only to discover that I've lost a boatload of money due to lazy record keeping.

I can bet on the wrong horse even with the right data.

I hate numbers, statistics and most of all - spreadsheets. That's why I hire people to help me with the math and make sure I get it right. It's not that I'm not good at math, it's that it's hard for me to sit down and work on spreadsheets.[1] I use tools and software to track and organize my numbers because getting your numbers right is not optional.

At this moment, you might think that you don't need to be serious because maybe this book won't work. Maybe this book will be like all the other business books you read in the past – while you were excited when you read them, you forgot them a week later. Those books didn't work so maybe this one will make you feel good, but it won't work either. Wrong – you have reversed the chicken and the egg.

It's because you never took those books seriously enough that they never led to success. I want you to realize that I'm already preparing you for success. When you master the Five Rings, success is an inevitability. So you'd better be prepared for that.

In case you are wondering which tools I use and recommend, don't worry about that just yet. I have an entire bonus section where I cover everything from this book on the Breakthrough page of my website at ServeNoMaster.com/Breakthrough.

If you're casual and blasé as you grow your business, you can end up investing in something that's losing money. I can't tell you how many early entrepreneurs shout, "I just made my first $1,000!" when in reality, they've lost more than $10,000. They want to have a win so bad that they only look at their gross profits, ignoring their net. They ignore how much money they spent on training, software, tools, consultants and everything else to get to that first sale.

The danger is that they'll keep doing the same thing.

The following year, they might think they made $10,000 when in reality they lost $90,000. I've seen businesses lose millions of dollars, and it's usually because they brought in a CEO with a good smile and a couple of good ideas who treated the company's money with disdain.

One of my favorite shirts I bought for my son says "Tumblr user."[2] I laugh every time because Tumblr is the perfect example of this. Tumblr is a blog site that makes no money. It's a platform for people who don't spend money online. They built a massive audience that never buys anything, so advertising on there doesn't go anywhere.

Yahoo! paid 1.1 billion dollars for Tumblr in 2013. It turns out the real actual value is almost $0.[3] All their users don't spend any money online; that's the exact audience you don't want to market to. Four years later, and Yahoo was no longer an independent company.[4]

People are really excited about cryptocurrency these days. Many of my friends are selling courses and training on how to be a master of cryptocurrency trading and become a bitcoin billionaire. That sounds very exciting, but if you enter that world, you can't treat it like a game.

I bought twenty dollars worth of bitcoin about five years ago when I was hiring people for some small tasks online, who would only accept payments in bitcoin. I created a bitcoin account, put $20 in it and spent $9. I forgot about what was left. Then the bitcoin craze happened, and suddenly, that nine bucks was worth five hundred.

If I had been a little more serious and treated bitcoin as a business instead of a hobby, I would have made a lot more money.

No matter what path you choose to follow, start treating it like a business. This book is your first expense. Until you make back the cost of this book, you haven't made any money.

## Reflection Questions

1. When you bought this book, did the money come from your entertainment budget or your business budget? (Do you even know what you paid for this book without flipping to the back cover?)
2. Are you expecting a financial return on your investment?
3. Have you started business projects in the past that you thought of as hobbies?
4. Do you spend money differently when it's for a hobby and a business?
5. Have you jumped on trends in the past just for a bit of fun?
6. What action steps can you take today to demonstrate that you have switched to the business mindset?

## Take Action

Start tracking your business expenses now. You can use one of the tools I list on my Breakthrough page, a notebook, or a spreadsheet. The tool doesn't matter so much as the practice. If you paid for this book, write that number down at the top of your ledger. If you use Kindle Unlimited and are reading this for free, consider putting your monthly bill on the ledger. You paid for this book one way or the other.

Keep track of each expense, no matter how small. I drink

hot chocolate rather than coffee when I work. I never drink it purely for pleasure, so that cost always goes on the business ledger. Your other business books, domain names, and website hosting should all be on your ledger as well.

Just writing down these numbers will shift you from a hobby to a business mindset.

## 15

# REMOVE FAILURE AS AN OPTION

When failure is an option, it becomes unavoidable. If you consider failure to be one of your options, you will never succeed. The reason we set vague goals that don't work and don't write them down is that we don't want to feel bad if we fail. If you start off saying, "I don't want this to happen if I fail," you've already killed yourself from day one. The only way to truly succeed is to remove failure from the options set.

In my previous books, I've told stories about Navy SEALs and how only the ones who succeed are those determined to either pass or die. But we don't need to be so intense in this book. Let's instead talk about *Monty Python and the Holy Grail*.

One of the greatest stories of tenacity is the story of the Black Knight. Though a terrible fighter, he never gives up. When he loses one arm, he refuses to give up and says, "Fine, I'll fight you with one arm." When it loses both arms, he threatens to kick his enemy. When he loses both of his legs, he says, "Come over here, and I'll bite you." The scene is hilarious, and it's also a great story because he doesn't give up. He'll do whatever it takes to win, and that should be your mindset.

Whenever the thought of quitting enters your mind, think of the Black Knight. It should remind you of tenacity and also put a smile on your face.

There are different ways to put yourself into a failure-proof mindset. When I started this business nearly a decade ago, I had no choice. I was fired, and the boats were burned behind me. I can never go back to the education sector.

### I am unemployable.

If I sent in a resume to every single Fortune 500 company, somebody who makes less money than me would inform me that I'm not quite what they're looking for – I am overqualified, underqualified, undereducated, overeducated, or I lacked the relevant experience. The funny thing is that if I approached those same companies as a consultant and asked for an exorbitant amount of money, their first question would be, "Where do we wire the cash?"

When you become failure-proof, your value goes up. Make a decision right now that you're going to succeed, you are going to go on this journey with me, and you are going to go all the way. If you make that commitment, you'll succeed. I have no doubt that this works. I've been doing this for a very long time. Not only do I teach this life, but I also live this life, and it's my passion.

Before we move on to Ring of Earth, where we're going to focus on the barriers that hold you back, I want to make sure your mind is in the right place. Ask yourself right now, are you ready to bleed with me? Are you ready to continue this journey with me?

To get your mind into the right place so you can accept more knowledge, you will need to be ready to:

1. Correct your mindset
2. Focus on real and attainable goals
3. Create systems that divide those goals into actionable steps
4. Treat your money with respect
5. Remove failure from the table.

When you feel comfortable with those five simple steps, you've completed the Ring of Wind. You now possess the mindset of success.

Congratulations on locking in your first superpower!

Each success, no matter how small, should be celebrated. I'm proud of you for making it this far, and if I was there right now, I would give you a high-five. Keep going!

## Reflection Questions

1. Have you already thought about reasons why this book won't work for you?
2. Do you think this book might work for other people but that you are the exception?
3. Has your company ever hired a consultant to do the same work as you but for a higher price?
4. Could you get paid more for doing the exact same work as an independent contractor, freelancer, consultant or coach than your employer pays you right now?
5. Are you ready to dig deep and break through some barriers in the Ring of Earth?

## Take Action

Make a commitment to stay the course. Most people who start this book won't finish it. And that's not just this book. Book completion statistics are abysmal, and I don't want them to get in the way of the life you deserve. Make a commitment right now to finish this book and put a deadline on it. This is a book designed to be taken seriously.

Make a commitment to complete all of the exercises and answer each question honestly in your Journal. Participation is the first step on the path to success. The more actions you take, no matter how small, the shorter the gap between you and success.

Write down your commitment in a public place. Add it to the sign in your bathroom or share it in the Facebook group. Just saying something out loud adds more power to it. You can build on this activity by setting a real goal to change your life and committing to that timeline.

# RING OF WIND REFLECTION QUESTIONS

1. Has your mindset been holding you back from the success you deserve?
2. Is there a part of you that hesitates to take action because you think you will fail so why bother trying?
3. Have you tried to set big goals and failed to achieve them in the past because they were overwhelming?
4. Does breaking goals down into manageable and measurable chunks make them a little more achievable?
5. Are you ready to remove failure from your language?
6. Are you excited to start tracking your money like a real business?

# 17

# RING OF WIND MASTERY

Although wind is the first element, it is by no means the easiest or least important. There is a reason that I call each element a ring. This process is circular.

As you grow and master each ring, you will go back to previous rings and see new layers that you never even realized were there. A beginner and advanced student will gain different lessons from the Ring of Wind.

As you experience more successes you will find your mindset shifts and coming back to this lesson will take you to loftier heights. Even with all my experience, I still need to re-focus myself constantly.

There are many projects that get me excited, but there is only so much time in each day. It's important to implement each of the activities from the Wind Ring and to really dig into the reflection questions.

Whether you keep a physical journal or store your answers on your favorite digital device, it is the action of writing down your answers that matters. When you finish reading this book, you will be able to go through your answers alone to track your journey.

One of the biggest dangers a new entreprenuer faces is forgetfulness. In six months, you might complain about days where you only make a few hundred dollars on the side, while right now that might seem like a massive success.

Tracking your progress will help you to remember where you started and maintain perspective on your success. At this point, I would encourage you to join my free group the Author and Entrepreneur Accelerator.

Every day I post new training and motivational videos, ask group questions and encourage discussions within the group to keep the motivation, encouragement and account-ability flowing.

It doesn't cost a penny. It's just a supportive community where you can ask any questions that arise from reading this book and get the answers you need in real time.

**ServeNoMaster.com/break**

# ELEMENT TWO EARTH – BARRIERS

# 18

## THE BONES OF THE EARTH

E arth is the element most associated with strength and powerful muscles. We think of this element as crude and brutish. It's the exact opposite of the nimbleness of air.

Mountains are huge, boulders can crush us, and caves are terrifying. While Earth is a powerful force, we have achieved dominion over this element. We build skyscrapers from the element of the Earth. We build military bases inside mountains. While we were initially intimidated by Earth, that has now changed.

Your mindset needs to catch up.

While earthen barriers may seem insurmountable, they are actually nothing more than dust.

In this Ring, we are going to dig deep into your psyche and root out the goblins living in the caves of your mind. Each of us has a very specific reason why we are living a life less than we dreamed of. I could interview every single person reading this book and ask the same question: "Whey haven't you built a passive income stream to support you through life and into retirement?"

I have done my best to answer every single barrier in this Ring. If, somehow, I haven't specifically answered your personal barrier here, you can probably intuit what I would say based on the dozens of other barriers we are going to crush through in this section.

This is the longest Ring in the book, so I understand if you skipped around and saved it for last. On the initial read through, you might just skip to the barriers that apply to you personally. That's okay. This section can be a choose-your-own-adventure if you like.

However you choose to tackle this section, get ready to get dusty because we are going to be breaking through a ton of barriers very quickly.

# 19

# THE GLASS CEILING

When I was eighteen, I went to a new club using a fake ID to get in. The bouncer was a big guy with dreadlocks and was very intimidating. He looked at the picture on the ID, looked at me and said, "This isn't you." Of course it wasn't. It was a friend of mine who'd given me his ID to pretend I was twenty-one.

I refused to back down and said, "What are you talking about? That is me. Are you trying to say that all white people look the same?"

He became flustered and said, "Whatever, man. You can go inside."

Walking inside, I realized they didn't serve alcohol at that club, and it was eighteen and up. I risked my brand-new fake ID over nothing. Nothing memorable happened after walking inside that club; the important moment was my first interaction with that bouncer. I'm still friends with him twenty years later, and he has an unbelievable tale.

My friend grew up in abject poverty, in a neighborhood where shootings were a weekly occurrence, and many of his relatives were in jail during our time together. He definitely had a great deal of experience on the other side of the law, but more than his criminal nature, what astounded me was his brilliance. As we became friends, I discovered he was younger than me. He just happened to be way bigger.

He was so large for his age that he was able to find work as a bouncer for a club that he could never legally step foot inside of. Over the course of our friendship, I discovered that he was a musical prodigy and could play five different instruments. He was the kind of guy that everyone was rooting for because he had managed to avoid the worst of the dangers of his upbringing.

But unfortunately, his mother had convinced him that he would never amount to anything. Despite multiple opportunities coming his way, he would always turn them down. One of our associates offered to pay for him to go to college, to give him a way out of his neighborhood. Another friend of ours asked him to be the manager of one of the most popular clubs in our entire city. Unfortunately, the only thing greater than my friend's natural ability was this lack of belief in himself.

He was a bit like a real-life *Good Will Hunting*, always carrying textbooks that he'd found at the local library in his backpack. He was passionate about studying and learning and yet, whenever an opportunity came his way, he would reject it. Not because he felt the job was beneath him, but because he was convinced that he wasn't quite ready yet.

Unfortunately, that still hasn't changed. His life is limited by a ceiling that's not actually there. If you get a jar of fleas and put a lid on that jar, they'll keep jumping and hitting the lid for a couple of days, but eventually, they will learn that it hurts. At that point, even if you take the lid away, they won't jump out.[1] I hope you enjoyed my bug metaphor, and now you get a little bit of taste of my Southern upbringing.

What was true for my friend is true for most of us. The reason I'm a successful author and ghostwriter and live on a tropical island in paradise is not that I'm smarter than you. I am not brilliant. It's not because I'm a better writer than you. You may have noticed that the words in this book aren't nearly as fancy as some of the stuff other authors write. A better writer would have used a better word than "stuff" there!

What does separate me is that I believe I'm capable of accomplishing anything I set my mind to. My belief that there is no ceiling above me is what drives my success.

**I believe in my very core that I can accomplish anything that I devote 100 percent of my focus to.**

When I started my first online business, my mentor told me that most people make the same amount of money their first year working for themselves as they did the previous year working for someone else.

My final job was working at one of the best universities in the world, and my salary was $36,000 a year. My first year working for myself, I made within 5 percent of that number. Every single month, whenever I hit around $3,000, I would stop. I had months where I made it the very first day. I would close a big deal, receive a payment for over $3,000, and take the next twenty-nine days off.

That was because I felt $3,000 a month was my value. I let someone who fired me determine my self-worth.

New entrepreneurs often believe that they are worth what someone else has told them. If your last job paid you $12 an hour, then you're inclined to believe you're worth $12 an hour. This is why many new ghostwriters and bloggers price themselves so low.

Take a moment to lock in to this concept. Would you like to make the exact same amount of money next year as you did this year, or would you like to blast through that barrier?

One of my friends is a very successful voice-over artist. We were speaking on the phone the other day, and he told me that the standard starting rate in his industry is $1,500 per finished audio hour. And yet, there are people out there who are getting paid $25 to $50 for the same amount of work. They don't value themselves enough, and it's a tragedy.

There's something inside you holding you back right now, and the core tenet of this book is to break through it. The Ring of Earth is all about barriers because each of us has a very specific barrier holding us back, and it has enough power to feel like a physical wall. By the end of this Ring, however, you will do more than just break through your personal barriers. You will destroy them without mercy.

As we work our way through the five types of barriers you might face, some of these might strike home for you, while others won't apply. I am going to cover as many different types of barriers as possible so that I will at least be close enough to help you overcome every single one of yours. But here's the secret. Every single barrier in this Ring can be boiled down to a single sentence:

$$\text{I can't do X because I have Y}^2$$

We're going to dig deeper and get very specific, but I want you to hold that formula in your mind. When we break each of our barriers down to its core elements, the formula emerges time and again. Those barriers that seem so different from the surface are all the same when you dig down deep.

- I can't move to another country because I need my high-speed Internet.
- I can't take my kids to another country because they couldn't handle changing schools.
- I can't quit my job because my family would lose our medical insurance.

We all have different excuses, and we can either see them as a reason to quit or a barrier that we can break through. The truth is you can blast through every single barrier in this book. Come on this journey with me as I take you through the six types of barriers that hold us back from the life we deserve.

# PSYCHOLOGICAL BARRIERS

The first type of barrier holding you back lives within your mind - mental barriers, beliefs, and limitations that we feel cannot be overcome. They're the most powerful barriers because belief is more powerful than reality.

It's a common plot in books and movies, where the characters get caught in a dark, marshy swampland and keep seeing threatening monsters until they discover that the monsters are coming from their own minds.[1] Whatever they think of ends up attacking them.

These movies are closer to reality than we give them credit for.

Just because a barrier is in your mind doesn't mean it's not real or powerful. But here's the beauty. These are all thoughts, and we can control them directly. When we break them out into the real world and face them, we can start to take away their power by saying their names out loud.

Let's examine the different types of psychological barriers.

## PSYCHOLOGICAL BARRIER #1 - I'M TOO DUMB

The first type of psychological barrier is the idea that you lack the intelligence to start your own business. Examples of this could include:

- I'm too dumb to start my own business.
- I'm not smart enough because I didn't graduate from college.
- I'm not a brainiac.
- I don't have the confidence to start my own business.
- I'm a follower, not a leader.
- I'm an introvert.

None of those things matter. You can easily hop on the old Internet and read about billionaires who never graduated from college, high school, or grammar school. You'll discover that some of the most successful people in history lacked a formal education.

The truth is that words have power, and the more you say you're dumb or any other negative word, the more those words gain power. This is something I'm dealing with in my private life at the moment. My wife is now running her own business. For so long, she felt the same thing – she wasn't smart enough, she didn't have the education, she didn't have the opportunities. But she's already very successful.

Our belief that we're dumb is often in direct contrast to our actual experience. The danger of repeating these lies to ourselves is that you start to believe it, and you start to act that way. Words have a great deal of power.

Some scientists recently performed a fascinating study comparing senior citizens in America and China.[1] In Eastern countries, grandparents are revered, and the thought of putting your grandparents in a home is shocking. Most families are dedicated to honoring their ancestors because their connection to the past is considered very valuable.

On the other hand, in America, we see our parents as a barrier and impediment to living our lives. As they get older, we can't wait to get them out of our lives. In the West, we believe that as you get older, your mind starts to weaken, and you start to lose your sense of self.

We expect those things as a part of aging. However, this study discovered that memory gets stronger as people age in the East. Their ability to handle tasks and play simple games improves rather than decreases. This is the difference between Western and Eastern culture. It's a cultural aspect, not a physical or intellectual effect.

It's the belief that your mind will weaken that causes your mind to weaken in the West. Belief is that powerful.

Every time you say you're stupid, you curse yourself. I want you to stop it right now, and here's a way you can train yourself. Whenever I discover a bad habit like this, especially a negative thought, I have a very simple system to make sure I stop immediately. Every time you catch yourself saying or thinking you're dumb, slap yourself in the face. The more it hurts, the more effective this technique becomes.

You can put a rubber band on your wrist and twang if you prefer. There is truth to the phrase: "Pain is a teacher." This is how you can reverse the undesired programming of your brain and kill that curse.

I'm not the smartest guy in the world. I can admit to you that I am unbelievably terrible at sudoku. If I had to solve a sudoku puzzle to save my mother's life, I wouldn't be able to do it.[2] I've tried children's sudoku, which only has six boxes instead of nine. I've tried sudoku games. I've tried sudoku with colors instead of numbers. It's just something I cannot do.

Just because I can't do one thing, does it mean I'm dumb?

Instead of pulling away from your weaknesses, you want to lean into your strength. Ask yourself, "How could I leverage what I'm good at and what I'm comfortable doing into a great success?"

Another thing I don't understand is bitcoin and blockchain technology. I'm constantly being asked to invest or participate in this industry, and I always say no because I don't understand it. I'm sure if I dedicated six months of my life to watching videos and reading books, I would begin to understand it. But rather than fight against the tide and try to learn something that baffles me, I lean into my areas of strength. And that's exactly what I want you to do.

Look at each challenge you face in every area of your life and ask yourself, "Is this an obstacle or an opportunity?" Whenever there's a sweeping market change or a shift in any of the industries where I do operate and feel comfortable, I see it as a moment for greatness. Everyone else is running away from the challenge, switching industries, or changing their business models, and that means their customers are there waiting for someone else, and that someone else can be me.

The book world is in constant fluctuation. Online bookstores keep changing their algorithms, constantly doing sweeps because people put out terrible books and fake reviews trying to manipulate the system. In this constant battle between good and evil, the bookstore's aim is to deliver to its customers the book they want. They want their customers to have a good buying experience, and they want every single part of that process to have integrity because that's core to their business model.

In this battle, there are often casualties in the form of independent authors who aren't actually doing anything naughty, but what they're doing is close enough to the naughty people that they get swept aside too.

They are collateral damage.

People freak out every time this happens - authors retire, and entrepreneurs who are trying to turn book writing into an industry disappear.

All their old customers come and find my books because I don't give up. I don't see obstacles. I see opportunities. Whenever someone puts a barrier in front of me, I say, "How can I turn this into a financial advantage?"

Less than two months before my third son was due to be born, our landlords gave us three weeks' notice. Instead of painting the nursery, we were packing our things up.

Our landlords chose to kick us out in a way that was less than classy.

Rather than the landlord speaking to me, man to man, his wife spoke to my wife. When I spoke to him and said,

"My pregnant wife is now bawling her eyes out. Why don't you just talk to me?"

He hemmed and hawed and refused to look me in the eyes.

I said, "We've lived here for two years. We've always paid our rent early. If this is a business decision, please speak to me like a man."

You'd think that after two years of paying the rent early, month in and month out, we'd get a little courtesy before they show us the door. But you can't rely on other people. Your strength needs to come from within. Real challenges are going to come your way, and if you don't deal with this psychological barrier now, it will creep up on you when you're vulnerable.

There was a moment where I thought, "It's time to move far away. I don't want to be on this island. I'm tired of people playing these games."

I want to be absolutely real with you. The pressure of moving and finding the right doctor for our son's birth was crushing me. It's not always financial issues that squeeze your mind. I started to think that I didn't have what it takes to make our life work here.

After a few moments of self-pity, I took a look in the mirror. This was just another obstacle. And when faced with an obstacle, there are only two choices. Give up or overcome.

Not only did we persevere and overcome that obstacle, but we now own and live in our own little hotel, which generates a great deal of revenue. In fact, there's a possibility that my wife will make more money than me next year. She might even make more than our old landlord.

**Take Action**

If "I'm dumb" is one of the barriers you need to break through, here's an exercise for you. First, of course, you have to slap yourself in the face every time you think you're stupid. I know not everyone will do that, but I can tell you that it works for everyone who does it.

The second activity is to find your avatar for strength. Create a version of yourself in your mind (it can be a fiction-alized character) that is who you wish you were. Every time you're in a situation where you feel too dumb, imagine that you are this smarter, more intelligent, more dynamic version of yourself. You will become this person if you keep acting like them.

This is a very powerful technique that I've used in many areas of my life, and it's led me to great success. Before you jump on to our next psychological barrier, take a moment to think about this one and create your character. I recommend that you pull out your Breakthrough Journal and write down a detailed description of this person.

If you're really serious about making a change, you can go beyond this and create a collage or draw a picture. The more senses you attach to this perfect version of yourself you're creating, the more powerful the process becomes. Those "I'm too dumb" moments will disappear. You will turn obstacles into opportunities and realize, "Oh my gosh, if I still thought I was dumb, I'd be missing this opportunity. But I won't – I know I can capture this one!"

# PSYCHOLOGICAL BARRIER #2 - LACK OF EDUCATION

I'm not a big believer in formal education. My children do not attend accredited educational institutions. I believe that more than 90 percent of our educational system in America is totally flawed, if not an absolute scam. Look at how many people working in minimum-wage jobs have college education or higher degrees.[1]

The majority of our education is wasted. I have a master's degree that I never use. A lot of people spend all of their time trying to put together enough money to send their children to college because they believe that's the only way to move them from middle class to upper-middle class. Of course, it's not true.

When you compare what university costs right now and what you get, it's ridiculous. Many people in their forties are still paying off college debt. What a great investment! For the same money, my parents could have let me start and fail with nine different businesses. Instead, when I graduated from college, the first job I had was working as a tutor for $14 an hour with no benefits and no guaranteed hours. I had to drive across town from job to job, and while I was driving, burning gas, wearing down my car and sweating through the back of my shirt, I was getting paid peanuts.

The founder of Wendy's, Dave Thomas,[2] never went to college. He was not an educated man, but with the simple idea of a square hamburger was able to launch a massive restaurant chain.

Most of the things you learn in school are not useful. In your career, you will most likely use less than 10 percent of what you learned in school.

When was the last time someone asked you to measure a triangle to save someone's life? I could write an entire book about how they don't teach things that are useful in school, but instead, I want to focus on real education.

Real education comes in small pieces, and it's focused. It teaches you how to have specific skills. Real education is a knife fight in an elevator. It's where you have to have the right bit of information about that very specific thing in order to accomplish your goal.

I have been in negotiations with people worth more than a hundred times more money than me. I've done business deals with billionaires. They have more money, education, leverage, friendships, relationships, knowledge, and experience than me. They have all the assets on their side, while I'm just a little vendor who ghostwrites for the occasional minor celebrity or wealthy person who wants to get their word out there.

When I'm in those negotiations, 99.9 percent of what I learned in school doesn't matter. None of it comes up. It all comes down to my ability to be smart about the tiniest of topics. I don't have to be smarter in every category. I only have to know more about writing, ghostwriting, telling stories, connecting with the audience, and getting books out there. All I do is tell that story and justify my price using a negotiating system that I certainly did not learn in school. That's how I built and forged my empire.

The book you're reading is educating you and giving you tools, knowledge, and resources that you wouldn't get at a four-year institution. American education is designed to take children, crush their creativity[3] and create cubicle drones at the age of twenty-two. That's not what I want for your life, and it's certainly not what I want for my children. I want to encourage their creativity and imagination.

The other day, my daughter's teacher told me that she's very sneaky. If she can get away with it, she'll win by cheating. I was proud to say she does not get that from her mother; she gets that from her father.

### My children play to win, and I don't care if they color outside the lines.

My daughter's kickboxing instructor puts colored cones all over the gym, and the kids have to run and bring back one of whichever color he shouts. This activity has one purpose: to make her tired. She has nearly infinite energy, and it rarely works. She'll run back and forth across the gym for color after color, never getting tired. She loves the game, but it doesn't change who she is.

If he blinks, she'll put a white cone inside another white cone and bring them back together. Not because she's tired or doesn't like the game but because my blood flows through her veins, and we play to win. Through her creative problem-solving, she tries to find a way around the rules. This part of her personality is exactly what most education in the West would try to tamp down, cut off or grind away.

This creative problem solving is the very trait I want to

encourage because it's exactly how I built my entire business.

The life we have is the result of my resisting formal education. The creative part of you is the most beautiful and brilliant thing within you, and we want to unleash that on the world because that's how you forge a beautiful business. Your lack of education is not a weakness. It's an asset. It means that you haven't been programmed too much. Untraining someone who has been taught the wrong way to do things is not an easy task.

There are some variations of this belief that rear their ugly heads as we get older. We can start to believe that our education is out of date or no longer relevant because society and technology have changed so much, but it couldn't be further from the truth. Whether you have no formal education or your degree is decades old, we are going to smash this barrier right now.

## Take Action

Track down five different people from high school or college. Examine their careers and see if there is a correlation between education and success. I promise you're going to be surprised by some of the results. You'll find many people who went to college and did nothing with their lives, and you'll find other people who didn't go to college but found their own ways to success. And there's more to life than just financial success. Owning your own small business, even if you make less money but have total freedom and no boss, feels pretty good.

Find out for yourself how important education actually is. Think about how education affected you. How much of your education are you using or not using? Take a moment to look for actual proof and stop relying on assumptions.

## PSYCHOLOGICAL BARRIER #3 - I WILL FAIL

A coward dies a thousand deaths; a hero dies only once.[1] I'm no hero, but I'm also no coward. I haven't died a thousand times – just a few dozen in my mind – but I love this statement because it's so true. If you keep telling yourself that you're going to fail, that fear will keep getting bigger. The truth is you are stronger than you imagine. The things you can endure are beyond what you've ever believed, and I'm going to prove this to you as we work our way through this process together.

When I was twenty years old, I was jumped by a pair of United States Marines[2] in a nightclub. I was at far less than my full faculties, and even if I had been at 100 percent, I am sure I would have lost that fight. They started in on me at the top of a flight of stairs. They beat me, pushed me down the stairs and beat me all the way down. Fortunately, after just a few minutes, club security came and pulled them off of me.

Here's what's amazing. It didn't hurt that bad. I don't say this because I'm a tough guy. I say it because how much I thought it would hurt was not the same as how much it actually hurt. We have this belief that failure of any kind, whether it's losing a fight or a business, will be unbelievably painful. But in reality, we go through these painful moments and rise up from the ashes stronger than ever before.

It's not victories that make us strong. It's failure that forges that sharpness. If you look at each of the moments in your life where you had a failure, something knocked you down, or someone told you that you couldn't do something and you fought against that, that's where you found your inner greatness – the strength that separates you from the rest of our society.

There are several ways to overcome the fear of failure. The first is to remove it as an option. You have to decide not to allow yourself to fail. Failure only exists if you stop afterwards. If you fail and then retire, that failure will define you for the rest of your life.

Have you ever thought about how many people who have run for president and lost, then run four years later and won? I bet you can't name one President from the last hundred years who lost and then won.[3] We don't remember failures as long as they're followed by victories. That's the critical lesson.

Don't let failure define you. Make a decision right now that even if you hit a wall, things don't go well, you have a bad day, or your first business collapses, you will not give up. You will keep fighting. If you remove failure as an option and quitting as a solution, success becomes inevitable. You have no choice but to succeed.

Additionally, humans are terrible at predicting the future. Here's one of my favorite exercises in the world to show you what I'm talking about. You can go into any scenario and write down what you think will happen.[4] I used to do this back when I was single.

I am terrible at talking to girls on the phone. I grew up at a time where I would meet a girl, she would give me her phone number, I would have to memorize it, call her house, speak to someone else who answered it, and then they would bring her to speak on the corded phone. Now, of course, we can text and send messages without ever having any meaningful communication. But back then, this was the system, and I was so bad it was astounding.

I'll never forget the girl I went through this entire process, including dealing with their brother, only to have her say "I didn't think you'd remember my number" and then hang up the phone.

Realizing that I was terrible on the phone but good at planning and writing, I decided to create a plan. I created a flow chart where I would write down conversation topics, questions, and every possible answer that she could give. All the different flow charts ended with me asking her on a date and her saying yes. That was the plan.

When I tried it out, every single time, we were off the chart within the first fifteen seconds. I was not willing to give up quickly, so I decided to adapt and overcome. Each time I ran into a surprise, I would write it down and adjust the flow chart accordingly. Here's something else I discovered. Surprises don't repeat themselves very often.

Try this game yourself. See if you can predict anything. You'll be terrible at it. Nobody knows how to predict the weather[5] or sports results. All the stats might say that your team is going to win, and then something happens, and they don't. On any given Sunday, any team can have their day and shine.[6] It's anybody's game.

**Worrying about failure is a waste of time and energy.**

I cannot predict 99 percent of what happens in my business. I can't tell you what's going to happen when a client calls me. I had a ghostwriting client email me a couple of days ago and ask for a phone call. I sent her a rough draft about four months ago and haven't heard from her since. Her email informed me that a lot of things happened in her personal life outside of her control, which limited her ability to work on the project.

In preparation for the phone call, I put together about ten ideas of what I thought would happen. None of those things happened. I wasn't even close.

I called up my insurance company the other day because they hadn't returned my phone call, and I was ready to go to war. I had prepared an entire strategy for that phone call, but the lady on the other end said: "Everything's taken care of. We're going to email you. Don't worry; you don't have to pay any extra fees. It's all sorted out. It was a mistake on our part." I was on the phone with her for less than thirty seconds. If you knew how much time I spent strategizing the night before, you wouldn't believe it. I was so upset I couldn't sleep. All of that effort, and I was dead wrong.[7]

Instead of fearing failure, see it as an opportunity to learn. As long as you approach every failure as a chance to get better, nothing will stop you from succeeding. My whole life, people have been telling me that I was a failure, I'd never amount to anything, I'd never succeeded starting my own business, no one would ever love me, and I'd never have children. Every category you can ever think of, people said bad things, and they probably said bad things to you too. We all went to high school with bullies, and people say mean stuff to each other all the time.

Guess what? I have a successful business, an amazing

wife, and amazing kids. That's the result of ten thousand failures and rejections. Do you think anyone looks at me and my kids and goes, "Man, I bet that guy got dumped a lot." But if you're wondering if I got dumped at prom, the answer is yes. Twice.

There's a reason my first blog about my dating life was so popular – I had a lot of tragedy. It's the same with business. I've been through almost fifteen different business models in the past decade. Markets have shifted, the business I've been in has shifted. I've had to adapt and change. I've been through big failures and tough moments.

But no one asks me how business was three and a half years ago. No one cares. All you care about is the "right now." Proof is in the pudding. Results beat everything else, and that's why you can fail your way to the top.

If you learn from your failures, you only become stronger. Success on the first try doesn't exist. Let go of that fantasy. Nobody knows how to ride a bicycle the first time they take off the training wheels. We all fall and end up stronger. I encourage you to continue to fail your way up.

**Take Action**

Write down ten predictions about the next seven days. It can be about anything and everything. You can try and make predictions about yourself. Write down in a sealed envelope what you think you'll have for breakfast the next seven days[8] or the first thing you'll do every single morning. You're going to be astounded by how wrong you are, even about the smallest things. This activity is going to encourage you because it will show you that your fear of failure is based on nothing, and you can let go of it.

## PSYCHOLOGICAL BARRIER #4 - I COME FROM A LONG LINE OF LOSERS

This is a tough one because it is not just in your mind. Sometimes, you look at the lives of your parents and relatives and think that's your future. It feels inevitable, but that feeling is just another belief that's holding you back, and we can break through this.

Every single one of us has a few losers in our DNA chain. More than a few people in my family tree were criminals, but why would I let someone else define me? I want you to think about how powerful this thought can be. If you are defined by your ancestors, and that means you can't be successful, then your children are trapped on the same train. You have cursed them.

You do not want to pass down this belief. That's why it's so important that we break through this right now. If you won't do it for yourself, you have to do it for your children. Don't you want them to have a better life? Every single person I know wants their children to have a better life than they had growing up. That's all I want for my children. And I want more for your kids, too. You have to make a decision to break the cycle, or the cycle will continue.

**The past cannot predict the future.**

Your parents' past cannot predict your future. There are many famous examples that discredit this belief. Oprah Winfrey was born to an unmarried teenage mother and lived in rural poverty. She would wear dresses made out of potato sacks because her mother couldn't afford to buy her clothes. She was molested by some of her relatives and their friends when she was nine years old.[1]

She had an awful childhood, but she didn't let that define her. She followed her dreams and became a millionaire at thirty-two. Now she has fans all over the world, and she is making history. The Oprah Winfrey Show is still the highest-rated daytime talk show in the history of American television. She wouldn't be where she is now if she believed that our past determines our future.

Katt Williams, a hilarious stand-up comedian I enjoy a great deal, was homeless for several years.[2] He fought his way out. He had a small talent that he grew. And there are plenty of other stories of people who have escaped poverty, bankruptcy, and terrible financial situations to achieve great financial success.

## Take Action

Track what happened to the five richest kids from your high school. I bet you can still remember their names. Think of the kids who had the deck dealt in their favor. If the success of parents guarantees the success of children, how come there's not one successful business name right now with the same last name as a tycoon from one hundred years ago? Where did they all go?

When was the last time you heard of someone with a

trust fund becoming a brilliant business owner or doing anything of value in their life? Coming from money and having everything handed to you on a silver platter usually leads to a weak personality. They've never faced adversity, so they don't know how to deal with it. You don't know how strong you are unless you get tested. People who've never been tested are at a disadvantage.

Take a few moments, hop on your favorite social media and look up all those people who come from a long line of winners and seemed to have everything in their favor. You'll see that a lot of their lives did not turn out that great.

# PSYCHOLOGICAL BARRIER #5 - IT'S
# TOO LATE

Colonel Sanders was sixty-two when he franchised the first Kentucky Fried Chicken,[1] and now KFC is everywhere. Chaleo Yoovidhya is a name you're probably not familiar with. But I bet you've heard of Red Bull. He didn't kick things off until he was sixty-one.[2] Laura Ingalls Wilder published her first book in the *Little House* series at sixty-five.[3] Gladys Burrill ran her first marathon at eighty-six[4] and set a world record running the Honolulu marathon at ninety-two. Alan Rickman was forty-two years old before he finally caught the acting break he deserved in the Christmas classic *Die Hard*.[5]

We all look for different excuses for inaction. I bet for much of your life, you thought you were too young to start your own business, and now, suddenly, you're too old. What's the perfect age? Was it a two-week window that you somehow missed where you were no longer too young and not yet too old?

The majority of my followers are not young, but they're amazing. I have people in their eighties who are starting their own businesses right now, and they're achieving success. They're writing amazing books, building blogs and learning how to use social media better than I am.

If you're not dead, there's time on the clock. The game is never over. It's never too late to adapt, grow and build a new business. I didn't write my first book until I was thirty. I was building an entirely different career that literally ended in a snowstorm. It's easy to look at your career and say, "It's too late to start a new career. You're deep into this one, you've got to stay here. Just wait. You don't want to lose that investment."

If you've put in ten years towards becoming something, you don't want to quit and start something else. The fear of loss is stronger than the desire for gain. Dan Ariely talks about this in depth in *Predictably Irrational*, another book that I love.

If you gave someone $10 and then took away $5, they'd be mad at you. If you walked up and just gave them $5, they'd be happy, even though in both cases the end result is they have $5. We are not rational people. That's why most economists are always wrong. They try to make predictions based on math and rational decision-making, but people don't act that way. Most of what we do is based on emotion.

No matter which way you look at it or what your reason for saying you're too old, you're not. It's not too late. It's never too late. Let's think about what it really means to be too late.

If you had six months left on the clock, what would you do? Would you keep doing exactly what you're doing right now or would you finally follow your dream?[6]

I was at a Dave Matthews' concert about a decade ago. I was sitting in the back of the field. He starts playing a song I haven't heard before, but I'm feeling the vibe. He begins singing the song, and I'm convinced the lyric says, "You might die tonight." I began to think, "There are quite a few people at this concert. There could be thirty or forty thousand people here. Someone might die tonight in a car accident or have a heart attack in the crowd."

**If you have a large enough crowd of people, tragedy becomes an inevitability.**

In case you're wondering, that's not the actual lyrics or name of the song. It's called *You Might Die Trying*. It's a song about how you should try instead of giving up, but I caught a different message. I heard what I needed to hear: you have to live the way you would live if it was your only choice.

If I had six months to live, 99 percent of the way I live every day of my life would not change. That's the ultimate testament. My father recently had a conversation with me about some of his regrets in life. He regretted where I went to college and a few of the other decisions I made earlier in my life. I responded with what I can best describe as a rage.

Bad stuff's happened to me in my life. Bad stuff happens to everyone. But guess what? If getting thrown down a flight of stairs by two Marines means I get to have my three awesome kids, well, let's go. Give me a toss.

The way I measure the quality of my life is not how much money I have, where I live, or how pretty my wife is. It is how much I would change it if I only had six months to live. And the truth is I would change very little. I spend most of every day with my son, my daughter, and my newborn son.

Bad things have happened, but I don't have regrets because I'm happy with where they led me. Stop worrying about the past. Stop saying it's too late. Instead, follow your dreams and passions and unlock the destiny you deserve. If you only had six months left, you could still write that great novel to leave your mark on the universe. You could still design your dream T-shirt or do whatever your absolute passion is.

## Take Action

Crack open your Breakthrough Journal and write down the answer to this question: what would you do if your life changed dramatically tomorrow? We can think about it changing in a few different ways. What would you do if you were fired tomorrow? What would you do if you won the lottery tomorrow? What would you do if tomorrow you found out you had six months to live?

What would you do if you found out you had forty years left to live and your entire retirement fund was gone?

Be honest with yourself because I've been honest with you. I write very personal things in my books because I know that sometimes the only way you can open up is if I do it first. As I told you earlier in this book, if you bleed with me, I'll bleed with you.

# PSYCHOLOGICAL BARRIERS
## REFLECTION QUESTIONS

1. Have you ever felt too dumb for a project?
2. Have other people convinced you that you don't have what it takes?
3. What curse word do you use to describe yourself? Is it dumb or something else? Maybe it's about your age?
4. Did you learn how to walk without stumbling? How about riding a bike?
5. Have there been big failures in your life that were on the road to success?
6. Have you developed skills and accomplished things in life where you originally thought you would fail?
7. Do you have members of your family who have set the wrong example for you?
8. How many of your friends and co-workers do you judge based on the success of their parents?
9. Is your psychological barrier stronger than your desire to improve your lot in life?

# PSYCHOLOGICAL BARRIERS ACTIVITY

We've covered a lot of psychological barriers, and I probably gave you some ideas for barriers that you haven't thought of. In your Breakthrough Journal, write down each psychological barrier that holds you back right now. Are there any that held you back when you were younger but no longer have power over you? List any barriers that you face that weren't included in this section.

Create a list of each barrier, how you will feel when it's gone, and how you intend to overcome it. Which strategies and exercises will you use? How will your life be different when you have shattered these barriers?

# FINANCIAL BARRIERS

E very single person in the world experiences financial barriers. In the past, you could go to prison for falling into debt. The rich could crush the poor to maintain their dominance. Technology, and especially the Internet, is the great equalizer. You now have access to knowledge, tools, resources, and allies that would have been impossible to reach just a decade ago. Wealth is becoming more accessible.

The real danger with financial barriers is how they affect your mindset or your time. When we separate the need to pay the bills from how it affects your mind, we can break through the barriers separately. When a big bill hits, it can crush you. You just want to lie on the floor, give up, and perhaps even declare bankruptcy.

While giving up seems tempting, it never improves your lot in life.

You can deal with financial barriers by developing a crystal-clear action plan using the activities in this section, and you can deal with the mental barriers using the techniques shared in the previous section. None of the financial barriers can actually stop you from writing a book, posting videos on social media, or finding freelance work online. While the problem might exist in the real world, the barrier is actually in your mind.

## FINANCIAL BARRIER #1 - I'M BARELY GETTING BY

We live in a society that has shifted dramatically over the past century from a financial point of view. Just one hundred years ago, nearly everyone in America had a nice little savings account to protect them. The banks didn't like this. They wanted access to all that currency to increase their profits, and that's why they invented the credit card.

With the development of the credit card,[1] we shifted from a society where everyone had savings to one where everyone has debt. Now we live in a constant state of financial stress where we increase our mounting debt by using financial resources that are even worse.

We start off our adult lives with a college loan that seems like a good deal until we're still paying off that 6 percent loan more than a decade later.[2] If things get a little bit tough, we grab a credit card to bridge our debt. If we miss a payment, suddenly, that interest rate balloons to 30, 50, or even 100 percent. It's merciless.

As things get tighter, you can no longer get more credit cards because you're behind and have to turn to payday loans, which absolutely gouge[3] you. Every single one of these proprietors will tell you that they're helping their customers 'bridge the gap' between what they need and what they have. In reality, this only causes us to feel like we're just getting by because we are in a constant state of financial pressure.

There's always a way to diminish your spend and strengthen your financial position, but it often means sacrificing, downsizing your house, or moving back in with your parents. This is not the type of advice we want to hear. I can't tell you how many people have failed to build a business because they did not want to give up their entertainment budget, whether it was buying video games, going to sporting events, or pounding drinks every weekend at the bar.

Moving back in with your parents is tough in your twenties (I know because I had to do it). But doing it later in life when you have kids? That's a real nightmare. The last thing you want to do is walk away from a mortgage you can't afford or downsize the home you spent so much of your life trying to move into.

We spend so much of our lives attaching value to objects and buildings that are constantly diminishing in value. By the time we realize we have lost that shell game, we have to move into a tiny apartment. Sometimes, sacrifice is required on the path to freedom. I spent eighteen months sleeping in hell so I could build my business from the ground up.

When I was just eighteen, and I was trying to figure out my first budget, everyone I talked to in college told me I should budget at least 80 percent of my income for entertainment. That is exactly how our culture works. Entertainment first and obligations last. We don't want to give things up.

I know some people are in really tight financial situations, but that doesn't mean you can't start to open up new revenue streams. Remember: this feeling that you're just getting by is purely psychological. It's just a belief that can be overcome by realizing that you don't have to be rich to write your first book.

Whatever business you're building, there are two main resources you will need: time and money. If you have no money, you will just use more time. I've had moments where my family was under great financial strain, when we were caught between a medical emergency and a housing emergency in the same month.

There was a moment where I was tempted to give up and stop working because of the emotional stress. And that is what we want to avoid. We want to separate the fact that we don't have resources from the psychological pressure.

No matter which type of business you want to build, you can pay with your time. There's a reason the very first training I send everyone to on my website teaches you how to make your first thousand dollars in the next thirty days without buying anything from me. Once a month, I get a message from someone who wants to put a course on someone else's credit card, borrow money to pay for it, or spread it across three different payment methods. I always say no. I'm not against making money, but I am against pushing people further against the fence. It's not necessary.

Their financial situation is often just an excuse because I provide multiple ways to gain access to every single program that I sell without them dipping into their savings or borrowing money from a friend. The first path is to go through my free training program, write a few paid blog posts for clients you find online using the exact system I outline and use that revenue to pay for one of my courses.

The second path is to begin to write reviews of all my

books and products. One person has worked his way up to my most expensive course with this system. Simply by writing honest reviews, recording videos and giving me powerful feedback, he received a $3,000 course for free.[4] The real problem isn't money; the problem is mindset.

Wealth is not a prerequisite for success. And that's why we want to break through the mindset that struggling financially means you aren't capable of building something new. As we get into the later elements, I will show you how to build multiple businesses without spending a penny.

## Take Action

Most of us approach our financial woes by putting our heads in the sand. It's easier to ignore the problem than to face it. To begin the breakthrough process, you must have a firm grasp on your situation. Start tracking your finances using software, spreadsheets, free programs online, or a notebook you keep with you at all times. Just knowing your numbers will start to reveal places where you can decrease your monthly costs.

Once you have a crystal-clear picture of your finances, write down your first goal. How much money do you need to generate from a secondary income stream to remove that psychological pressure? Once you have a fixed goal in mind, it becomes achievable.

# FINANCIAL BARRIER #2 - STARTING A BUSINESS IS EXPENSIVE

We often hear that starting a business is expensive. There's no other way to say this: it's just not true. As you'll see when we go through several business models in a later section of this book, there are dozens of ways to start a business for less than $100. When I grew up, the rules were different. The standard belief was that to start a small business, you began with a loan for $25,000 from the bank.[1] Those days are behind us, but some people are stuck in that mentality.

I remember when I was trying to teach an associate my online business model. Back then, she could have made a huge amount of money by entering a market where we had a big opening. Unfortunately, she missed the boat. Her dream was to take a business that was more than 90 percent profit and use it to build a bricks-and-mortar business where, in a good year, you would generate 3 percent profit. That means taking an investment of $100,000 and hoping that you turn it into $3,000 each year.

**When people are trapped in ancient mindsets, they get ancient results.**

In the Void Ring, I will share with you six actionable business models that don't require a massive investment upfront, but first, it's time to let go of ancient business models and beliefs. You can break through with research. Everything you learned at university, you can learn online. The Internet has become the great equalizer of knowledge and information.

Smart businesses now can be entirely self-funded. You can build a business that generates revenue from nothing and use that first revenue to pay for growth. I don't believe in debt financing. It's not necessary. It's a trick perpetrated by those old greedy monsters that run the banks.

Don't fall into the mistake of thinking that you need to raise money to start your business. You don't. Build a business from the mindset of, "I must generate a profit or I don't eat," and you will discover a completely different way of operating. It is a completely different business model.

If we remove external funding and debt funding from our mindset, suddenly, we discover the ability to form lean start-ups. I built Serve No Master from the ashes of my past career for a measly $500.

When I started out, that's how much I invested in my first training course. That's all it took, and I believe that's still far too much. That's why I want to teach you how to do it spending nothing. Big investments are not necessary.

## Take Action

Your mission is to break through the inaccuracies in an effort to find the truth. Look at the six business models covered in the Void Ring:

- Writing books

- Creating online content
- Buying and reselling services
- Printing on demand
- Setting up deals between product owners and people with followings
- Recommending products you believe in

In your Breakthrough Journal, write down these six business models and how much you think it costs to get started on each of these paths. It's critical that you write down your guesses now, so that when you reach the end of this book, you can look back and compare your beliefs to reality.

So many of our financial assumptions are based on third-hand information. Become someone who always looks up the numbers before making a decision.

# FINANCIAL BARRIER #3 - THE BANKS WON'T LOAN ME MONEY

I've been involved in a lot of projects over the last decade. One of them, which I can't go into great detail about for legal reasons – because at the end the knives came out – started with a great deal of investment. Significantly more than the five hundred dollars I used to build my own personal business. That experience was the confirmation that cash-rich businesses make poor financial decisions.

If you're not sure what I mean, go to Silicon Valley and visit any business one week after they receive a round of funding. It's ping pong tables in the break room and Teslas in the parking lot for everyone. They've gotten a taste of the big number.

It reminds me of rock stars in the eighties and nineties when they signed a deal for an album. They would get massive amounts of money, and suddenly it was new cars for all their friends and new houses for mom before the first song was written.

I don't believe in risking massive amounts of capital to build a business. That's not what this book is about. This book is about going from zero to one, not from one to ten.

It's about building your first revenue stream, not acquiring and accelerating another revenue stream. It's a very different mindset and a very different business model.

Running businesses from the front of a boardroom and letting your minions handle all the small pieces is not what I do. That's not who I am. That's not what I teach. I'm a street fighter. The way I build a business is a knife fight in an elevator.

One of the greatest lines in any movie of all time was by Val Kilmer in the movie *Spartan*. He meets a Special Forces lady and says, "What do you do?"

She says, "I teach knife fighting."

What he replies is bit dark but brilliant: "You need to stop teaching knife fighting and start teaching people how to kill, so that when they meet someone who took a knife fighting class, they can send their soul straight to hell."

What he says there is the embodiment of one of the core principles of *The Book of Five Rings*. You don't fight and practice to win with a particular move. You don't train to win with a hard strike, a soft strike, or a strong strike. You only train to win. And that's what you're going to learn as we break through this mindset.

It doesn't matter that banks won't loan you money. Banks don't deal with people like us because we don't need debt anyway. Lean start-ups that begin with small money and bootstrapping are far more successful.[1]

Here's something else that often gets lost in the noise coming out of the tech start-up world: most of the people who start a business and raise tons of money to grow quickly end up owning very small percentages by the end. If you own 1 percent of a business that sells for a million dollars, you'll make less money than someone who owns 100 percent of a business that sells for $20,000.

Don't get caught up in the hype. Focus on what you can do. Stop focusing on the obstacles. A bank won't loan me money right now either. I'm completely and totally unhireable. If I were to send out my resume to all around the world – social media, SEO, and online marketing and building businesses – I would get a barrage of rejection letters. It's very hard to explain that I've been out of the "standard" workforce for eight years.

It only matters if *you* think it matters. I haven't thought about or been tempted to send out a resume in years. The thought of working for someone else ever again disappears completely once you realize how successful you can be with your own business, on your own terms.

**Take Action**

Complete this book and write down the real numbers it will take you to get started online. How much money do you need to start a blog, launch a podcast, or write a book? There is no excuse for complaining about money until you know how much you need.

Once you have a clear figure in front of you, develop a plan to raise the capital you need. Can you cut back from your entertainment budget for a few months or take a part-time job? Switch your mindset from excuse-creation to problem-solving.

Make a commitment to find a way to overcome each obstacle and to never let finances be an excuse ever again.

# FINANCIAL BARRIER #4 - I'M IN DEBT

So is most of America. The purpose of our business model is to decrease debt rather than increase it. That's why we don't want to borrow money from banks. That's why we don't want to max out credit cards. That's why we don't want to buy things we can't afford. Our approach is going to be the approach of the grappler – getting close, getting dirty, and getting a little mud and blood on your shirt.

The traditional business model and the traditional economic system of the West has failed you. You've been let down. I'm very highly educated, and the only value I get from my education, which cost hundreds of thousands of dollars, is complaining about how worthless it was in books like this one. That's the only thing I use the majority of my education for.

The thing about debt is that it's not real. It's not a physical thing. You can't touch a debt. You can't hold the debt in your hand. It's an artificial construct of our society. You can only feel the results of debt, and most of those results come in the forms of stress and emotional pressure.

Being under debt feels like there's a mountain on your

shoulders, and that can affect your ability to do anything. You can feel like your hands are tied. But when you realize that this possible financial problem is actually psychological and separate the two issues, things are very different.

I've had moments where I was scared, even in the past few years. Last year, my son needed major surgery. As we went into the hospital, I discovered that they wouldn't take my insurance. As I was bringing my son in, my insurance company informed me that they only pay afterward. They won't pay upfront or help at a single hospital in the entire country.

That situation was stretching me to the limit to pay for expensive medical care. Surgery on an eighteen-month-old is expensive and terrifying. You don't want to cut corners. You don't want the discount doctor or the discount hospital.

I thought I'd done everything right. As my son was wheeling off to have surgery the next day, I was crying. He was leaving in my wife's arms with a little hat on and the IV in his hand. A nurse comes into the room screaming, "Stop the surgery! Your son has pneumonia. If we give him anesthesia, it will kill him."

I don't know the right words to describe how I felt in that moment. I wish I were a better writer so that I could describe what it feels like to be that close to losing the only thing that matters. And I wish that was the only time something like that happened to me.

A year later, my insurance company changed underwriters and promised that things would go smoother. My second son was being born. There was an emergency, and my son made it through his birth by the skin of his teeth. He was within five minutes of not making it and my insurance bailed on me again.

When you're in these moments and realize that your

financial preparations might not have been enough, it's very scary. You can either collapse or make the decision I made: to be a knife fighter.

When it comes to business and family, I'll do whatever it takes. I am 100 percent a mercenary. When I say that I'm a ghostwriter, and I've made a lot of money writing books for other people, that means I'm a pen for hire. As we've all heard, the pen is mightier than the sword. Thus, I'm even more dangerous than a gun for hire.

That's what we do. We don't let financial pressure or the threat of debt crush us. We say, "I'm not giving up." I want you to capture that mindset because it's the exact opposite mindset of most of our culture.

Most of our culture is looking for an excuse to give up. You can break the fear of debt mindset by chopping it up into small pieces and using small goals and commitments, such as, "I'm going to decrease my spend by stopping these activities." Sometimes, it takes a little bit of sacrifice.

To build my business, at twenty-nine years old, I moved back into my mother's basement. I celebrated my 30th birthday living in that pit of despair. If that isn't a mood killer, I don't know what is. I lived in my mom's basement for a year, building my business to the point where I was above minimum wage.

It took me a year because I didn't have what you have right now. This book is the book I wish someone had handed me when I was just starting out. I fought my way out of my mom's basement.

And I moved into my friend's apartment. And when I say moved in, I mean I began sleeping on the couch. I lived on that couch for another eighteen months. It was brutal. For two and a half years, I was in the dirt. But one day, at the end of that entire journey, I was making enough money to split a two-bedroom apartment with my friend. And I slept in a bed again.

## Take Action

Take a practical look at your financial situation. Does your debt preclude you from the ability to work? Or is it simply affecting your mental state? We don't live in a society with debtors' prisons anymore.[1] While it can feel like you have to work your tail off to just get back to zero, the effort will be worth it.

While it's outside the scope of this book, work on a debt reduction plan. Just having a plan in place will reduce a great deal of that emotional burden.

Once you have separated the practical challenges of debt from the emotional barrier that is holding you back, go back to our psychological barrier section and begin to implement those strategies to get your mind back on track and focused on the business you are going to build and use to break through your debt barrier.

# FINANCIAL BARRIER #5 - I STINK AT ACCOUNTING

I'm very bad at numbers as well. If I could go back in time, I would un-take all of my advanced calculus and physics courses and take statistics instead. I used to know how to solve the equation for shooting a rocket in your backyard while standing on a merry-go-round during an earthquake. Really useful stuff.

I'm terrible at spreadsheets and statistics. Fortunately, spreadsheets are a skill, not a talent. It's something that is learned, not something you're born with. And it's something that you can overcome with a practical solution.

You don't have to change who you are. You just have to make a decision to overcome that barrier. There are multiple ways to do this. You can bring in a bookkeeper, get a partner who's good at numbers, or you can start using a spreadsheet and learn how to do it yourself.

It's very tempting to bring in a trusted friend or a sibling, maybe even the spouse of one of your siblings, to handle your numbers. But it is not the best solution. It's okay to have someone who's in charge of organizing your numbers, giving you the data to look at and helping you organize it into your structure.

It's not okay to give that person the ability to spend your money.[1] That's a whole different ballgame. I encourage you to invest time in learning money management. I am still learning and improving myself.

By now, you should have noticed that the majority of these financial barriers are only barriers because they affect your mindset. In the rare few cases where it's a real limitation, you can overcome it with software, training, or help from an outside source.

## Take Action

Research options for learning to manage your money better. You can find a list of accounting training programs and tools on the Breakthrough page of my website. Start with something simple that feels intuitive to you. The first step in this process is to start keeping records.

Choose a tool to start working with now and follow this process. Every day, try to become a little better at accounting. If you can do better today than you did yesterday, eventually, you will become amazing.

# 24

# FINANCIAL BARRIERS REFLECTION QUESTIONS

1. Do you feel mentally trapped in a cycle of debt culture?
2. Do you buy things to feel good and then forget that feeling a few days later?
3. Do you actually know down to the pennies how much it would cost to start your dream business?
4. Why do we make decisions when we aren't even sure what they will actually cost?
5. Would you rather own a tiny percentage of a large business or have complete control of your destiny?
6. Would owing your bank a bunch of money for starting your business increase or decrease your stress levels?
7. Does having debt in your life limit your free time or hamper your ability to invest time in building a new business?
8. Are your financial barriers really stopping you

from investing in yourself or have they just poisoned your mind?

# FINANCIAL BARRIERS ACTIVITY

If you are in a poor financial situation, you can improve it with a three-step process.[1] Begin by creating a clear picture of your financial situation. Track and analyze your debt, obligations, and spending patterns. With that information in hand, look for opportunities to take control of your debt. If you can stop the hemorrhaging, you can start to get back in control of your life.

Once you fully understand your financial situation, develop a plan to turn things around. The lessons of this book are designed to be a part of that plan. If money is tight, you are going to absolutely *love* the Ring of Flame. In that section, just like a spreading wildfire, I will show you how to make money *fast*. I know that sometimes the enemy is at the gates, and you just need a little breathing room. I'll show you how to get it.

# 26

# REAL-WORLD BARRIERS

S ome of the barriers that hold us back are outside of your control. You can't control where you were born any more than you can control your native language. It's easier to see these barriers as made of steel because you didn't make them. They didn't start in your mind, and they aren't your fault. However, the Serve No Master philosophy has a core principle:

**No matter the cause, you can take responsibility for any obstacle in your life.**

Responsibility is not the same thing as blame. Instead, you are taking back your power. You are making a decision to change something even if you weren't to blame. Instead of feeling guilt, you should feel empowered.

You now have the ability to change your life, rather than spend all day complaining. You can break through.

# REAL-WORLD BARRIER #1 - MY ENTIRE COUNTRY IS POOR

This can be a real limitation. I now live in a country where opportunities are few and far between. My wife grew up in a way that most of us could never imagine. Your definition of poverty is her definition of wealth. Her favorite toy as a child was a rock. I know that might sound like a joke to a lot of people reading this book, but it's not.

She fought her first wild animal for survival when she was six years old.

Most people who read this book have never even pooped in the woods. In the West, we come from a place of such abundance that we don't know what it's like to be a real survivor. As much as I say that I'm a knife fighter when it comes to building my business, when it comes to raw, pure survival instinct, I'm not in the same league as my wife.

Poverty can be a real limitation, but there are ways for people living in poor countries to raise themselves up and overcome lack of education and access to resources. I am going to give you some tools that you can use to break through that. If they work here, they will work just about anywhere.

Each different country has different challenges, so you need to be agile, look at every single limitation that's unique to your situation and say, "How can I overcome this particular challenge?"

One thing I've discovered is that the poorer the country, the greater the prevalence of Internet cafes. And they're very affordable in these locations. In these parts of the world, almost everyone in there is playing video games. They use the computers and the Internet access they're paying for to buy escapism – trying to get their minds out instead of their bodies.

This reminds me of the movie *Ready Player One*, which I hate. I find the main character in that movie despicable. On the core level, he stands for everything I don't. He believes that you should use the Internet and online games as a way of escaping your situation and to imagine you're somewhere better, in a world of fantasy. I believe in the exact opposite.

**The Internet is a tool that you can use to escape poverty.**

Our approach to this barrier is going to be tackling it piece by piece. You might be from such a tough situation that you can't afford an Internet cafe. That's okay. There are places that provide free Wi-Fi.

There are so many resources if you are willing to be creative. McDonald's provides free Wi-Fi in every single one of their restaurants around the world. I'm not the biggest fan of the food they provide, but I am a fan of how they give an opportunity to everyone.

In 2009, I didn't have access to the Internet. There was a problem with my apartment, and it was a whole rigmarole. For three months, I couldn't get any Internet in my home, so

I would go to McDonald's every single day and work for hours.

There are local libraries with complimentary Internet access as well.[1]

You can make a decision to be agile and willing to overcome the different hurdles you face. Every piece of education you need is available online. Everything you need to make real money is available for free on my website.

In the country where I live right now, the average living wage is $100 a month. If you follow my free training, you can earn up to $1,000 a month. That means you make more than ten other people combined. You can live pretty close to like a king here for that.

If you're limited by your native language and your ability to communicate or interact with people, you can start by building small online resources for local businesses. This is how I started.

You can build websites for small businesses in your country for very small amounts of money. Because you are climbing the ladder, what you charge now will not be what you charge in a year. You'll grow from small businesses to large businesses, from local campaigns to national campaigns. Eventually, this will unlock international doors, and you'll begin to make real money.

The entire world is now connected online, and 99 percent of what holds people back these days is no longer physical; it's mental. It's the way they use the Internet.

Every single person I know who struggles to make ends meet on my island still has access to the Internet 24/7. They just spend all of their time online reveling in escapism rather than looking for a way out. I don't judge them. If you're happy with your lot in life, then you should absolutely live in a way that brings you joy. But if you're reading this book, you want more, and I want to unlock that for you.

## Take Action

Create a list of the barriers caused by your current environment. Are there real barriers holding you back? Are there certain payment systems you don't have access to? Is Internet access spotty at best?

Create an action plan to overcome each individual barrier. I can record videos, write books and even blog posts without Internet access. I only need to go online to upload all my work. Are you sure you need to be online all the time?

Dig down deep, analyze your barriers and see how real they are. Make a list of these barriers in your Breakthrough Journal and write down how you will tackle each one. When you break a barrier down into smaller pieces, it becomes more manageable.

# REAL-WORLD BARRIER #2 - I WORK TWO JOBS

This is really a time barrier. Whatever the source, not having enough time is a real barrier, but it can be overcome. I know exactly what it's like to be squeezed for time.

Being squeezed for time and feeling like there's not enough time in a day can become a real hurdle. If you're physically at two jobs throughout the day, and then you come home and want to spend time with your kids, I don't want you to stop doing that. I know what that's like.

My wife is in the middle of starting her business. Every single day, I help her work on her business when the sun is up, and then I spend all night working on my business. In between, I spend as much time with the kids as I can. We're fortunate that we own both businesses we're building, but it's still a great deal of time pressure.

If you're in this situation, the first thing is to make a decision to look for solutions, not obstacles: "I have this barrier. How can I overcome it? How can I creatively find a path to generating more revenue?" The first two things you should consider are cost control and ways to increase efficiency. Is there a way to decrease how much money you're spending in order to give yourself more time?

Depending on your family and financial situation, some options are possible, and some are not possible. I've seen a lot of business owners sell their house, put all their money into a business, and then move back in with their families.[1] If you're working two jobs a day, and moving back in with your family for six months will give you the runway you need to set down that second job and have the time to start building something else, then that's something to consider.

Sometimes, we have to do things that are uncomfortable in order to realize the things that we need and desire for our families in the long term. On the path to success, there's often a requirement for sacrifice, whether it's in your leisure time, entertainment budget, or living situation. You have to ask yourself, "Am I willing to give up certain things in the short term to provide my family with better things in the long term?"

We're often so busy living day-to-day that we have trouble looking at the bigger strategy. I encourage you to take a moment to look at it and say, "Is there a better way for me to approach my current situation? Is there a way for me to take slightly more control?"

If you absolutely can't change your living situation – if you're not spending money on entertainment, and you need those two jobs just to cover rent and food – let's look at another way to adapt. Can you leverage your relationships to unlock more opportunities? Can you put your kids to work?

I have loads of training on my website about how you can teach your kids to design coloring books that you can sell online for free. These can generate real revenue for you.

We can pass on skills to our children so that our financial barriers don't become generational.

The most important thing to do is focus on building your buffer, which is the space between you and debt. It's the amount of money we have to protect ourselves from financial shocks. By building your buffer, you create more breathing room, and you can get to the point where you can remove that second job.

Even better, use one of the many courses I have for free on my website about networking to leverage yourself into a promotion or raise so that you can make a little bit more money.

### Take Action

Assess your schedule analytically rather than emotionally. In your Journal, write down how you spend every minute of the next two weeks. Is your schedule really maxed out, or are you investing time in front of the television "decompressing?"

Look for areas where you can be more efficient and strategic with your time. If the solution cannot come from using your time more effectively, it can come from improving your financial situation.

Write down the exact amount of revenue you need to generate each month in order to leave the second job.

Focus on that as your primary goal. Even if you only have one hour available per week, you can use that time super efficiently to generate revenue. I'm constantly sharing places on my website that are paying for freelance work. And every single business model in the Void Ring can be implemented away from home. You can build your business from anywhere.

## REAL-WORLD BARRIER #3 - MY IDENTITY WAS STOLEN

This is an exceptional situation, but it does happen to people, and you can lose access to the financial resources you're used to. In this scenario, I would encourage you to create an isolated business ID – a business entity that's separate from your identity that's been stolen – while you work your way through that nightmare problem.

You can start out your business taking cash. That's exactly how my wife's business is starting. We're an entirely cash-run operation while we build her financial instruments. Because she comes from a poor country, they have a terrible financial infrastructure. It's very hard to get access to the most basic of banking assets. While her identity hasn't been stolen, she has similar limitations. It might be more than a year before she can start taking payments online.

There are loads of new financial tools developed specifically for people who come from developing countries. If you lack access to credit and efficient or trustworthy banking, there is always a way to overcome this challenge. You can connect your business to a prepaid credit card, so the only revenue you can spend is the money that comes in from sales.

This forces you to be a lean start-up. The good news is that the business models I teach will work even if you don't have access to any financial resources. That's why this method is so powerful. When I first started making money online, the first revenue I made was a check someone handed me. I haven't seen a check in a long time. But it's a still way to get paid.

No matter what your challenge is, you must look for solutions and say, "Okay, this happens. It stinks. How can I overcome?" Bad things happen to everyone. As much as I can try to prepare you for every single potential bad situation, I can't. You have to create a simple mindset. And I hope that from seeing these practical examples, you develop this specific mindset: "No matter what happens, I will look for a way to overcome it."

## Take Action

Make a decision not to let an external force, and especially a criminal, limit your future. Develop a practical plan for recovery, create a separate business identity, and create a list of financial resources you have access to. If you can't process payments, there are services that handle everything and pay you via direct deposit each month.

# REAL-WORLD BARRIER #4 - I WENT TO JAIL

Working for yourself is the one place where your past doesn't matter. There are many marketers who use their humble beginnings as part of their sales story. Watching someone turn it around is compelling. We always want to root for the underdog.

My record is not perfect. A little over a decade ago, I was applying for every sales job I could find – everything from selling used cars to mortgages – and at every one of these businesses, I failed the psychological test.

Looking back, now I realize I failed the "drone" test. They were looking for the ability to call people who don't want to hear from you, offer them a product they don't need and can't afford, and pick up the phone to call the next person when that one hangs up on you. The last thing they want in that position is an independent thinker.

I was sitting next to someone performing the job while I was taking one of these tests, and I had to listen to him make the most mind-numbing cold call in the world. He would call business after business asking to speak to the

CFO and then offer to make a free presentation on money management to his entire staff. His pitch was awful. He was trying to find a company that would let him target their staff for some sketchy "financial services."

I'll be honest. The name of this company is very similar to one of the largest and most respected financial institutions in the world. The name had tricked me into showing up for this job interview. Only about halfway through did I realize I was in a boiler room.

Shockingly, I failed their psych test.

It asked questions like, "Would you rather be more renowned for your skills with paperwork or your skills with a copy machine?"

My first thought was that if I was renowned for either of these things, I'd contemplate taking my own life. I can't think of anything worse than being famous for being good at using a copy machine.

It reminded me of an old Michael Crichton book entitled *The Terminal Man*. In this book, they developed a pacemaker that was supposed to shock and reset the man's heart every time he started going crazy.

They gave him a psychological test, and one of the questions was: "Would you describe yourself as green or yellow?" They were analyzing the answers to see where someone was on the spectrum of insanity. Try to guess which color means you are more insane.

The way American businesses try to hire employees resembles the tests in that book. They hire people based on CVs and data. They try to figure out if someone's good for the job based on their level of education, what kind of grades they got, how many years of experience they have, what psychological profile corresponds to them, and whether or not they can pass a drug test.

I don't know how educated any of my employees are. I don't know how old they are. I don't care.

Can you do the task? You're hired.

You cannot do the task? It's not a good fit.

I run my business based on one thing: performance. And that is why my lean business is very successful.

Many businesses in America ask a lot of questions that don't matter. "Did you tweet something offensive when you were thirteen years old? Well, then, obviously you can't work as a carpenter because what you tweet affects your ability to hold a hammer."

As much as we say, "Once you've served your debt to society, it's gone," that's not true because it's on every job application. A criminal record can become a crippling limitation.

While I've never been to jail, many of my friends have. And they face a world where there are no opportunities because everyone they meet immediately finds out that they went to jail. Once you've been convicted, that's how everyone perceives you, and it's very hard to escape that perception.

Building your own business is the one place you don't have to check that box.

You're in the one place where no one gets to judge you. Your customers will only care about the quality of the work. Eventually, your story of escaping prison (not literally) and building something where you can become a positive member of society will become your selling point.

Your dark past can become the number one reason people want to work with you.

One of my followers has an amazing story. He grew up in a family in La Cosa Nostra, but he didn't want to be a part of it. When he got out of jail, he began to write amazing fictional books based on real stories from his life. He built an entire business around exactly who he was.

No one's going to hire you when you're from a very well-known crime family. But people will read your book. Look, how many people have read the book or watched the movie *The Wolf of Wall Street*. That guy now sells a program on how to be really good at sales, and people buy it all day long.

He was a full-on villain who ripped off the most vulnerable people in our society. And now he's revered as an anti-hero.[1]

The beauty of the new world is that you can use a pen name and build a new online reputation. I write under six different pen names. I'm not secretive about them, but you can be. The key is to focus on the future and say, "My past does not determine my future. Where I come from does not control where I'm ending up."

The beauty of working for yourself is that there are no tests. No one is there to judge you based on an arbitrary set of requirements that have nothing to do with whether or not you can effectively perform the position for which you're applying. You can escape from your past with a dedication to building yourself a future.

## Take Action

Make a decision to change your path and learn from your past mistakes. You can work as a freelancer and use any of the business models in the Void Ring without ever filling out a job application. When you're working online, people care far less about your past. There is a big difference between hiring someone online and letting them into your home.

Look at what financial instruments you have access to and where you need to adapt. Once you decide to move forward, it's just about taking the practical steps in front of you.

## REAL-WORLD BARRIER #5 - I DON'T HAVE A COMPUTER

I received an email from someone in this exact situation a few weeks ago. They had an extremely small budget for a computer, and we had a detailed discussion about the bare minimum that they needed to be able to start working.

In reality, you can start from nothing and make this your first goal. You can gain access to other resources and assets through alliances and creative problem-solving. Most libraries let homeless people come in and hang out all day long. They'll certainly allow you to sit down on the computer and do your own work.

You can create a Google account, so you always have access to everything you're working on, no matter which computer you're using. You can find a friend who has an old computer they don't use anymore.

You don't need a new computer to do what I do. You don't even need a computer to do what I do. I write my books without using one. I dictate everything because of my crippling eye medical problem. All I use is a phone and a $65 microphone that I clip to my shirt.

For every problem, there's a way over, around, or through. Old computers are absolutely fine. You can use a computer that's twenty years old to do the majority of what I do. You can use Open Office instead of Microsoft Office; it's free.

Some of the business models I'll teach you don't even require a computer. If you are good with your phone, you can be a social media manager just using your phone. There are tons of apps that allow you to use your phone for pretty much everything you would do with a computer.

There are loads of people out there with limited resources, but they can still do cool things because most online technology is shifting away from programs and towards apps, away from computers and towards mobile. To run her entire hostel, my wife is using a laptop that I stopped using a year and a half ago. She simply doesn't need a newer or more powerful one.

There's always a way to overcome these physical barriers with some resourcefulness and creative thinking. If you are facing a barrier I didn't include here, and you can't think of a way to overcome it by using the right mindset, send me an email. I'll find a solution for you, and I'll update this book to add that in. Look for a way to overcome your barriers and don't let anything hold you back.

**Take Action**

Create a plan to get access to the tools or resources you need. If you don't possess a computer, find a local option where you can gain access to a machine. Look at libraries, schools, and other educational institutions. Is there an affordable Internet cafe nearby?

Your first step is to find a way around this obstacle, and

your second is to raise enough money to eliminate it forever. If this is your barrier, price out a computer that can handle your needs without breaking the bank. A used computer from a pawnshop can probably get the job done for pennies on the dollar. Be willing to solve your problems creatively.

# REAL-WORLD BARRIERS REFLECTION QUESTIONS

1. Has anyone in your country ever escaped the bonds of poverty?
2. Why do they deserve a shot at a better life more than you?
3. Are you willing to do whatever it takes to create a better future for yourself?
4. Is your problem insurmountable or is it perhaps just your belief that's holding you back?
5. Are you willing to break through your beliefs?
6. Do you judge people by their past or their present?
7. Do you deserve a second chance?
8. Are you ready to turn things around?
9. Is lack of access to equipment holding you back or the belief you have attached to that lack of access?
10. Have you looked for creative solutions to the equipment you lack?

## REAL-WORLD BARRIERS ACTIVITY

S
it down and analyze your real-world barriers. Take a look at each one that applies to you. Divide your solution into two parts. The first part is your beliefs, and the second is practical limitations.

Write your list down in your Breakthrough Journal. For each barrier, create a plan for getting over your false mental beliefs. You have loads of exercises and activities from the previous sections that will work perfectly here. Now actually do those exercises!

For the practical side of your barrier, take real action. Find out what you need to do to find free time, access world markets, and get paid online. No barrier is real unless you test it. Don't be a flea that just assumes the glass ceiling is there!

# SOCIAL BARRIERS

S ome barriers come neither from within nor from society at large; they come from the people closest to us. As much as our loved ones want to support us, they often are the ones who clip our wings. They hold you back not because they want to stop your dreams, but because they are afraid you will fly away from them.

It can be hard to pull away from those closest to you, but many successful entrepreneurs have a story like this. Many of my friends from my twenties have faded out of my life, not because I pushed them away, but because they pulled back when I succeeded. They felt that I had "lucked into" success that I didn't deserve.

It can be a painful part of the process, but you can learn from my experiences. These are not insurmountable barriers. As you will discover in this section, yet again, the majority of the limitations are on how you let these people affect you. It's nothing to do with the actual power they have over you.

## SOCIAL BARRIERS #1 - FAMILY

Family can be the best and worst thing to happen to each of us. Before we look into specific family situations, it's important to understand some universal principles about humans.

As a rule, people don't like change. We go through phases in our teens where we rebel and want to change the whole world. In our twenties, we begin to find ourselves, and in our thirties, we want everything to stay the same forever.

I'm thirty-seven years old, creeping towards thirty-eight, and I don't like new music. I still like music that came out in the mid-nineties, and that's how most people are. We become dinosaurs. As we age, we like stability. And when we face things that are unfamiliar, it can become a big struggle.

This is why my life is so foreign to many people. The thought of moving to a foreign country and building an entire life far away from friends and family is baffling to them. And that's okay because I'm following my heart. I'm living my dream.

People who don't like change often have misconceptions about the costs, challenges, dangers, and dynamics of living in a foreign country. While there are some challenges as far as medical care and transportation, the majority of the things people believe will be challenges aren't difficult for me. I've found ways to deal with them. Often, the benefits outweigh the costs.

When people meet you for the first time, they judge you and lock you into a specific definition. Anyone who met me when I was in my twenties and kind of lazing around will always see me that way. People who meet me for the first time now see me in a completely different light. But your family, unfortunately, will always see you the way you used to be.

My family and siblings struggle to perceive me as a patriarch. I'm a man with children who leads his family. I spent my twenties traveling around the world and living a very casual, fun-filled lifestyle, trying to figure out what I wanted to do with my life, and resisting responsibility in every turn.

Now I live by the motto of the villain in *The Queen's Poisoner*: "Duty binds me." The responsibility of giving my children a better life controls every decision I make. But people who know you from the past will always see you as the way you used to be.

When you start to change, they are afraid of that change, and you can become trapped by their ancient mindset. Family members see us in certain ways, and that preconception will often color their perception of your desire to change your life. Your children may think that you're too old to learn to build a business online and will assume that anything you try will fail. They see you as the person you were twenty years ago, and they can't imagine you changing later in life.

Whether you are in your twenties or your golden years, it's important to approach family very carefully. I often talk about making loud statements to force yourself to hit specific goals, but you may be in a situation where your family is your greatest risk. In that case, I encourage you to keep your mouth shut until you've transitioned.

When you're going through a massive life change, such as building a business, if you know your family will say bad things, don't tell them until you've had some success. Give yourself a little bit of runway.

It's not about keeping it a secret. It's about waiting until you can give them the proof before they hold you back. It's about realizing that they come from a place of love. They're afraid you'll fail, and their fear keeps you from success. You have to decide that your life and the life of your children is more important than how the other members of your family feel.

## Take Action

Analyze your family situation carefully. Will they actively sabotage your work efforts or simply not understand what you are building? Have your parents or your children already decided what they want for your life? Will your spouse be terrified if you leap from the "security" of a job to the freedom of entrepreneurship?

Decide on the best course of action for your unique situation. We have a thriving and supportive community where you can connect with other people in similar situations and get custom advice.

Every family is unique. However, the best solution is often to work until you have a success. Once you can show that your idea is actually working, it's far easier to bring your family into alignment.

## SOCIAL BARRIERS #2 - FRIENDS

I went through a time of great transition when I decided to go from being terrible with women and alone to learning how to have social connections, talk to people, and have a better life. When I went through that transition, there were a lot of friends who held me back and said, "Why are you trying to change? What are you doing?"

It was a time of great tumultuousness in my life, and I learned a lot through that experience. During big transitions, you're very vulnerable. If your friends keep telling you that your business idea or your dreams won't work, eventually, they will clip your wings.

Be prepared for that. You can either not tell your friends until you're ready and have some success, or you can prepare a way to tell them so they can get in alignment with you.

They are going through a phase where they believe they're going to lose you. When two people are friends and one becomes wealthy, the friendship goes under a great deal of strain. There's a mistaken belief that the wealthier person will begin to think they're better than the friend who earns less money.

That fear causes the person who is not changing to over-react and often puts pressure on the relationship until it eventually fractures. Their fear breaks the relationship, not the successful person's pride. You have to assure your friends that it's not about leaving them behind but about improving your future and creating a world where you can do better things for your friends and family.

You're in a place where you'll have a different set of priorities. One of the big challenges will be when your friends encourage you to join them and do something that involves spending money or wasting time when you need to be working. I can't tell you how many times I stayed home on a Friday and Saturday night, grinding on a project until dawn rather than going out with my friends, seeing a movie, or having a drink.

You have to sacrifice your entertainment time and budget when you're building a business. The difference between yours and your friend's priorities is what causes friction. It's simply because you're pursuing two different paths, not because one of you is right and one of you is wrong. The danger is that enough of this peer pressure applied to you correctly will stop you from succeeding. You need to be prepared to resist that.

You are the average of the five people you spend most of your time with. If you spend your time with people who have no desire to make more money and are happy with their jobs, they will continually pull you down simply because that is the nature of humanity, not because of who they are as individuals.

If you surround yourself with people who are happy to rely on the government to provide for their retirement, they will pull you back every time you try to set up a new revenue stream.

If you surround yourself with five people who make twice as much as you do, however, they will pull you up through the same social forces.

## Take Action

Pull out your Breakthrough Journal. Assess your relationships analytically. Are you investing time in relationships that will lead to the life you want, or are you investing in friendships that are fun in the short term? While it's fine to have relaxation and entertainment time, separate that from the time you invest in your new business.

The more time you spend around people on the same path as you, the quicker you'll get to the top of the mountain.

Proactively look for people who are where you want to be. Try to find a local meet up, support group, or mastermind for entrepreneurs. Just spending an hour or two a week with people who understand where you are coming from and believe in you can offset the pressure to quit you may receive from your existing social circle.

## SOCIAL BARRIERS #3 - CO-WORKERS

We tend to think of our co-workers as allies. We think of them as partners and people that we're on the same journey with, but it's often not true. If you stormed out of your office tomorrow and said, "Who is coming with me?", how many of your co-workers would follow you?

If you tell your co-workers how you're building your own business, you'll put yourself in a place of vulnerability. You might lose your job. I encourage you to keep your mouth shut because you can find yourself in quite a predicament.

In addition to keeping your mouth shut, do not use any work resources to build your own business. Do not write blog posts from a work computer. Do not use a pen from work or a piece of paper for work. If you read the small print on your contract, your employer owns anything you create with their resources.

I remember the contract I signed when I was selling computers for one of the largest companies in the world. I noticed a section about "anything done on work computers we own" which basically said, "If you write a book on one of our computers while you're at work, we own it." Guess what? I never did one millisecond of work on those computers. It makes you vulnerable.

Work is the only glue that ties you to your co-workers. No matter how many promises you make, when you change jobs – whether it's starting your own business, working from home, taking maternity or paternity leave, retiring, or just going off to follow your destiny – those relationships fade away.

Because we know this is coming, I encourage you not to invest your emotional secrets with them because there's no upside, only downside. It can put you in a dangerous situation, and they might hold you back or even actively sabotage you.

**Take Action**

Make a commitment to yourself to get the support you need from a mastermind group, whether it's local or online. You can get feedback and support from people who believe in you and understand business without risking your primary revenue stream.

## SOCIAL BARRIERS #4 - I SUFFERED FROM A TRAGEDY

Tragedy can be painful. I've been through some tough moments in my life, but plenty of people have been through tougher. My best friend died in a car accident when I was still in high school. It hurt real bad. Some of my followers have been through situations that are far worse.

While I've had some close calls with my children, I'm very fortunate that they're still here with me. But I know that not everyone can say that. We have to get to a point where we decide whether or not we're going to be defined by our past and whether we're going to live the lives that those we've left behind would want us to lead.

My wife does not have a high level of education, but I put her in the position of having to run a business to provide a level of security for my family. If something happens to me, my family will have a place to live and a revenue stream no matter what. This hostel is my life insurance.

It's hard if you've gone through something especially painful, but our emotions are simply thoughts, and we have the ability to control them. If you're in a moment of great depression, but your house catches on fire – the alarm goes off and you smell smoke – you will stop thinking about that emotion and go into survival mode. You will activate different parts of your brain, and you'll forget that thought for a little while.

I've written several books on depression. If you're going through a time of tragedy, I encourage you to read those books where I deal more specifically with that topic. But I want you to know that process is the cure.

Rather than looking at the big picture, build a series of steps to get you through each day. Focus on each little piece, one at a time. When you're focusing on a small step, it takes up the totality of your mental bandwidth, and it pushes the pain at bay for a little while.

## Take Action

Take some time to assess your situation. If the roles were reversed, would you want your loved one to keep going, or would you want them to suffer forever? Loneliness can be very painful, but try to look at the other side of the coin. I know that if something happens to me, I want my family to keep going.

You may need extra time to recover from the pain of your loss, but look for a way to leverage that pain into action that your loved ones would be proud of.

# SOCIAL BARRIERS REFLECTION QUESTIONS

1. Does your family want what's best for you?
2. How would you feel if a member of your family started a career you didn't understand and worried would end in failure?
3. How does the thought of working on a project before telling your family make you feel?
4. Will your friends understand why you want to change your life?
5. What will you do when you have to choose between going out for "just one" and staying home to work on your business?
6. How does the thought of sacrificing time with your family, friends and coworkers to build your business make you feel?
7. Do you want your tragedy or loss to define the rest of your life?
8. Is there a way you can leverage your pain into motivation? A way to share your story and help other people?

## SOCIAL BARRIERS ACTIVITY

**A**nalyze your social barriers and separate the real ones from the emotional ones. There comes a time when you must take responsibility for your destiny. Are you ready to break free from people who are holding you back from a better life?

Find a supportive group of people who are on the same path as you and, ideally, slightly further along. Commit to meeting with this group for an hour once a week to brainstorm and support each other.

I can't tell you how powerful it is to have a group of people who just listen without judgment and understand what you're trying to accomplish.

# KNOWLEDGE AND SKILLS BARRIERS

Y ou might feel like you're a step behind the rest of the class. If you are missing a core skill, it can hold you back from the rest of this book. In some cases, it's time to face that missing skill directly. There are two ways to deal with each of these barriers; learn how to do it or pay someone else to do it for you.

If you are stuck at skills that are not in this section, these techniques will still work. Remember that you have a supportive community that is ready and willing to help you achieve your dreams. It is often shame that holds us back with these barriers. We are afraid to admit our weakness in order to receive help.

You are never too old to start a new business or learn new skills. Many of the skills that we find the hardest to learn are actually commodities. We can easily find someone to handle those tasks for us.

The good news is that the Internet is the great equalizer. You can now access the skills and training you need without having to tell anyone in your personal life. I have a list of loads of amazing places you can further your education on the Breakthrough page of my website and, of course, we are always happy to help you grow in the Facebook group.

## KNOWLEDGE AND SKILLS BARRIER #1 - I DON'T KNOW HOW TO READ

There are many reasons why reading English might be a barrier for you. Whether you grew up in the West or not, there are loads of people who can't read English well or effectively, including my wife and many of the people I work with. It's quite possible that English is your second, third, or fourth language and that, for whatever reason, you lack this particular skill. One would think quite easily, "Oh, this is a prerequisite. I could never succeed with a business until I mastered this skill."

The first question I ask you, of course, is: are you actively working to improve your ability to read? That tells us right away how you're approaching this challenge. Is it a barrier or is it just an excuse? If you give me a reason why you can't build a business, but you're not actively working to overcome that particular barrier, that tells me it's just an excuse. It doesn't matter whether English is your second, third, or fourth language.

There are loads of people who come to America or England as foreigners and make a conscious decision to master the local language. Just as there are many people who, instead, choose to stay in an enclave where everyone speaks their native language. They never assimilate, never learn the local language and become limited because of a decision they've made.

You could easily learn everything I have to teach without the ability to read. You can listen to audiobooks and watch training videos. There are loads of software tools that blind people use that provide text to audio. You can use these tools to read websites to you. Your phone will read text messages, emails, and websites to you.

The ability to read is no longer the prerequisite for business that it was fifty years ago. I dictate all of my books, and you can do the exact same thing. Rather than attempting to bridge the knowledge gap yourself, you can use software or a person to bridge the gap in the form of a transcriber or transcription software.

Your choices are to learn and overcome the barrier yourself or to use either a person or technology to bridge the gap. When you make one of these decisions, the inability to read is no longer a barrier. It's simply a step along the path to success.

There are loads of missing elements in the modern education system. Whatever piece of education you're missing, you can access that knowledge for free online. There are loads of free training programs on websites and YouTube that will teach you basic math skills, basic spreadsheet skills, how to read, and how to learn a foreign language. Anything you need to learn that's a remedial skill, you can make a decision right now to start learning that skill.

Don't let this be a barrier when it doesn't have to be. You have access to everything. You can teach yourself.

**Take Action**

Develop a plan to overcome your linguistic hurdle. Focus on business models from the Void Ring that don't require you to master this skill.

Analyze your current reading level. How long would it take you to achieve mastery? Is that a reasonable timeframe, or does it make more sense to focus on growing your business and bypassing this need?

Explore tools and resources that can help you bridge your language gap. This is the same strategy that you can use to enter other markets where you don't speak the language perfectly.

# KNOWLEDGE AND SKILLS BARRIER #2 - ENGLISH ISN'T MY FIRST LANGUAGE

Whether you can't speak English effectively or just have a heavy accent, this can be a limitation. There are several ways to deal with this issue. The first is building a business in your native language. You don't have to build a business in English. There are a lot of amazing opportunities in other markets.

Don't discount your native language. One of my friends is making a killing in the Brazilian market. The cost of advertising is much lower, and the competition is not as fierce. Our hostel recently received an email from two people who have traveled the world for eleven months without spending a penny because they have a travel blog in Catalan – a language only spoken in small part of Spain that every once in a while agitates for independence.

It's a very small subset of a small nation. Yet, two people found a way to build a following and an entire business. They've given themselves a nice living and a nice business because they started by focusing on their core language.

Many non-English markets are underserved, and that provides you with a great opportunity. One of the members of my mastermind makes most of his money online with books that are not in English. He translates every book he writes in English into four of the romance languages, and the money just rolls in.

His books are so popular that Amazon runs ads on his behalf all the time on Facebook, generating massive volumes of sales, all because he focuses on the languages where there's the greatest opportunity. There's far less competition in German, Spanish, French, and Italian than there is in English. Smaller market also means less competition.

You can also get serious about learning English. Most of the people I know who struggle with English never tried very hard. You're capable of great things, and if you want to master English as a language, you will make it happen. I have seen people do this.

One of my friends came from a foreign country speaking no English, taught himself everything, and you wouldn't even know he wasn't born in the West. He did all of this with no money, no teacher, no support, and no network because he was desperate to survive. He accomplished great things through drive and dedication.

Your third option is to hire out. Finding native English speakers is easier than you think. There are loads of people graduating from universities with degrees in English who are making no money. If you go into any coffee shop in America, there is someone there with a degree that they paid six or even seven figures for who are making minimum wage serving coffee. Guess what? They speak really good English.

You can hire an editor or an assistant whose job is to go through your books, products, or any of your work and clean up the English for you. It's easy to find these people.

Right now, it's a buyer's market, so the leverage is in your favor.

**Take Action**

Take a look at opportunities in your local market. Could you replicate an English business in a foreign language? Combining your knowledge of worldwide business practice with your local expertise could turn you into an unstoppable force.

Compare how long it will take you to overcome your accent with the price of hiring an actor to handle all your voice work. Be as objective as possible when looking at the pros and cons of each path for building your business.

# KNOWLEDGE AND SKILLS BARRIER #3 - I'M NOT TECHNICAL

I often receive emails from readers struggling with the complexity of the Internet and the pace at which technology evolves. When we get older, some pieces of technology can become overwhelming for us. But the beauty of the modern world is that you can always hire someone to fill in the technological gap for you.

When building a business, you should focus on leadership and process. Once you develop a process, you can hire someone to do the micro steps to accomplish that process.

I designed a strategy for how I wanted to grow my Facebook group, and I knew I couldn't do it myself. I hired someone to handle the technical aspects. This is how I deal with most social media because it's outside my technical know-how.

Whenever you find a gap in your knowledge, you have three ways to deal with that problem. The first is to teach yourself. When you do that, you pay with your time. The second way is to find a tool or piece of software that bridges the gap or makes it easier for you. There are tools that help manage social media platforms and make it easier to blog, upload photos, and email your audience. The third way is to pay someone else to do it. Your choice is between investing your time or your money to overcome each hurdle.

Rather than focusing on your weaknesses, focus on your areas of strength. If you are really strong in just one area, you can leverage that into growing a business. You can start by selling that one skill as a consultant. Use that to raise enough money to hire other people to fill in the gaps where you're weak. Now, you have a complete skill set between what you can do and what you can afford to hire out.

The easiest way to overcome the tech hurdle when your budget is low is to find a technical intern online. You can hire them at very affordable rates. Many of the things I find very challenging online when it comes to programming websites or doing social media tasks are actually affordable because so many people know how to do them. There's far more supply than there is demand for these skills.

When you bring a student on board as an intern, you train them in exchange for their labor. You provide the content, the strategy, the big picture, and all the things that come together to generate the revenue, and they simply manage the technology where you're not skilled.

I've run loads of interns through my business. Young students these days know how to tweet and hashtag but don't know how to generate revenue from it. The skill of technology is becoming a commodity. Rather than seeing it as a barrier, you should see it as one of the cheapest things to pay for online.

**Take Action**

Create a list of areas where you lack the technological wizardry to accomplish a task. For each of these areas, research possible solutions. Is there software to speed up the process? Are there local classes that can teach you how to use the tools? Are there local students desperate to transition their love of the Internet into an actual revenue stream?

Next to each area where you are weak, write down how long it would take you to master the process on your own and how much it would cost you to fill that gap with software or an employee. In the Rings of Water and Flame, we will build on these answers.

# KNOWLEDGE AND SKILLS BARRIER #4 -
# I STINK AT MATH

The good news is you're not in school anymore, and all the things that weren't allowed in math tests in high school are allowed now. You can use software, spreadsheets, calculators, and every tool you can imagine. Your inability to do math no longer matters.

My wife is not natural at math. Her underfunded public school didn't even offer math as a subject, so you can't blame her for struggling with math. If nobody teaches you, how are you going to learn? She never saw her lack of math education as a barrier or limitation, but simply as an obstacle to be overcome. She began to teach herself basic math by writing down all of our family expenditures. Whenever we would get into an argument about money, she pulled out her notebook and could show exactly where every penny went that month.

She now runs her own business, which takes in payments through wire transfers, cash pickups, direct deposits and of course cash. While she still doesn't feel comfortable using spreadsheets, she uses the hotel management software to track all of our incoming money. She still tracks all expenses in a notebook and she can tell you where every penny went every single month since we opened. She knows how much we have to pay all of our staff every month, where the money's coming in, where the money's going out, and how much money we can afford to spend on growth. She taught herself how to do all of these things.

You can use a calculator, you can use software, or you can hire someone else to do all the math for you. There are loads of amazing tools designed to help the mathematically challenged to take control of their finances.

To succeed with your new business, you just need to stick to the basics. You don't need calculus or algebra. All of the advanced math that I took was such a waste. I don't use any of it.

Triangles never come up in my business.

Math only comes up in my business when I'm tracking ins and outs and how much I can afford to pay people to help me on a project. I only use math in the real world when we are measuring a room inside our hotel to see if we can put in a piece of furniture. If I don't have a tape measure in my hand, I am probably not using any math. All of that trigonometry was a waste - triangles never come up because nobody owns triangular furniture.

My mastery of equations does not help my business.

The inability to do math is almost irrelevant for business growth. When I first started my business, I had no idea how to track ins and outs. I had no accounting software and didn't do any of the math correctly. I made loads of mistakes in my tracking systems, but I still succeeded. I focused on more core expertise, which was increasing how much money my fledgling business generated.

Whenever I wouldn't have enough money, I'd work

harder to grow the business to make up for that mistake. As you are starting out, you can do the same thing.

If you're strong enough in one area, it can make up for massive weaknesses in other areas.

Just work on developing your math skill over time.


**Take Action**

Math is about far more than just money. Every month, I have to track how many people visit my website and what percentage of them join my mailing list. I then keep track of how many people who join the mailing list make a purchase.

All of these numbers become percentages that I use to determine if a part of my business is working or something is going wrong.

There are some amazing free courses on the basics of spreadsheets and what they can do. I encourage you to start sharpening your math skills, as this will come up again as your business grows.

# KNOWLEDGE AND SKILLS BARRIERS REFLECTION QUESTIONS

1. How has your inability to read held you back from your dreams before?
2. Is it better to conquer this mountain or find a way around it?
3. Have you overcome technological hurdles in the past?
4. Is it too late for you to learn new things?
5. Do you have value that you could exchange with a young internet-savvy millennial for their skills with social media and the digital world?
6. Do all online business models require digital expertise?
7. Can you do well as the largest fish in a smaller pond?
8. Are there international markets that are currently underserved?
9. Have you assessed how much time or money it will cost to bypass your unique hurdles?

# KNOWLEDGE AND SKILLS BARRIERS ACTIVITY

C rack open your Breakthrough Journal. In the Ring of Water, we are going to dive deep into your strengths. This is a chance to start early. Create a master list of every area where you feel weak or lack confidence. With each of these areas, list possible solutions and how much they will cost you in time or treasure.

We can choose the best solution later in the book; for now, we are just gathering more puzzle pieces.

# PRACTICAL BARRIERS

S ome barriers start in our bodies, not within our minds. Often, our society discounts the disabled and assumes that if one part of your body doesn't work, the rest must be the same. You do not have to be defined by your limitation. You can leverage the rest of your assets into an unstoppable force.

There is no reason to believe that you can't succeed. You've made it this far, and I have great faith that you can accomplish anything. We live in a time where you can build an entire empire online without people ever seeing your face or hearing your voice. Whatever your limitation is, whether I have listed it or not, there is a way to work around it and achieve the success you dream of.

## PRACTICAL BARRIER #1 - I'M BLIND

This is the barrier that cuts closest to the bone for me. I have problems with my eyes. If you've read some of my other books, you know that my vision is one of my greatest challenges.

Eighteen months ago, I thought I was going blind. I sat down with my wife and said, "We need to make a strategy for how I can continue to support this family if I lose my vision." It was a very scary time for our family. I'm very fortunate that I came out the other side. I still have my vision, though problems with my eyes persist. I now run my business in a way that it would continue to operate successfully even if I were to lose my vision.

There are lots of ways you can overcome this challenge. Most people who are blind learn to read using Braille, the language you can feel with your hands. In addition, there are loads of software tools, as I mentioned earlier, that will read to you from a computer screen. There's loads of technology out there designed to make the digital world accessible to people who have disabilities, impediments, and disadvantages.

As part of this process, I recommend that you simply focus on viable business models that work for someone with your limitation. There are loads of things you can do online that don't require the ability to see. You can write books, tell amazing stories, create awesome audiobooks and videos, all without the ability to see. However, if you want to get into day trading, where you have to look at loads of data on a screen - that will be a lot harder.

Lean toward the business models that match your skill set rather than trying to fight against them and make things harder for yourself. You can do amazing things as far as coaching and writing books instead of trying to go down the path of web design.

When I was first starting online, I had a client who was legally blind. He was about 98 percent blind, so he wasn't totally blind. He could see shapes and colors. He had an idea for a website. I remember this client very well because he's one of the worst clients I've ever had. He told me about his vision for a website.

Because I was desperate to pay a bill at the time, I took the job, even though I shouldn't have. The job was to design a website that was a combination of Facebook and Sugar Daddy dating. He had this picture he'd found online of a man holding a bunch of hundred-dollar bills and making the shush symbol with his finger in front of his mouth. He would constantly tell me, "Make the money bigger. Make the money bigger. Make the money bigger."

To build out this website, I hired a team of web designers. The client gave me a list of what he wanted for his website. He had a template he was working from that he wanted to be modified. I got a price from a team. I tripled the price because I knew there would be some extra elements and extra challenges. He agreed to that price, so we began the project. Along the way, we had a lot of problems. Every time he would call me, he would say, "Hey, I'm so happy with your work. Everything's approved. You can pay out the team. Project done." Then, he would call me two days later and say, "Oh, actually, my friend looked at the website, and we want a bunch of changes."

He was trying to design a website that he could never actually see, and that's really hard. He did this to me not once but twice. I ended up losing money on the project, in addition to him calling me two, three, and even five times a day, constantly approving the project, letting me release the team I had hired, and then changing his mind, forcing me to rehire a new team. I ended up hiring two completely different design teams to do two phases of the project because he changed his list of demands.

This was one of my early projects. When researching to prepare this book, I was surprised to discover that website no longer exists.

I learned a lot of lessons about making it very clear what someone's paying for and that, once they approve a project, it's done. But I was just beginning back then. I was caught in the middle of a project with someone who did not mean to be demanding. He was paying for something he couldn't see.

Rather than leaning into your disability, lean into your strengths. Work on the types of projects you can still do. I can tell you right now that, if my vision went all the way out again, I would focus far more on course creation, audio narration, and books than I would on the design of my website. I would continue to generate blog posts, but they would be audio files I would send to someone on my team to transcribe, clean up, and add to the website.

There are some amazing things you can do online as far

as working with music as well. You have so many powerful things that you can do. Lean into those strengths, and you can accomplish great things.

**Take Action**

In the next Ring, we are going to dive deep into all of the things you can accomplish. While blindness is certainly a limitation, it's not nearly as limiting as it was in the past. You can accomplish amazing things without using your eyes. There are plenty of brilliant blind singers and writers.

Start building out a list of your skills and talents. Make a list of businesses that you can build without needing to see anything. Additionally, do you have a partner, teammate, or employee who can fill in the gap? Someone who can post the blog articles you write?

As always, we can bypass each of these barriers or find someone to fill in the gaps for us. Start building a plan that lets you move past this barrier as quickly as possible.

## PRACTICAL BARRIER #2 - I'M DISABLED

Stephen Hawking was massively disabled, yet everyone knows his name. The deck was dealt against him, but he didn't let it hold him back. He's considered to be a genius, one of the great physicists of our generation, making guest appearances on television shows and even in movies. He made the news all the time during his lifetime. He never let anything hold him back.

Of course, there are plenty of inspirational movies like *My Left Foot*, where someone learned to paint when they were very limited physically. Whatever your disability is, there's a piece of technology or someone you can hire who can fill in that gap for you.

I know that when something bad happens to you, if you've been through a traumatic injury or an accident, there's a period of adjustment. That emotional adjustment period is very painful and difficult, and I certainly don't want to discount that. What I want you to see is that, while it might feel like an emotional barrier, that's all that it is. You can still overcome it.

Whatever your physical limitation is, there's a way to

overcome it. If you approach it that way, you will discover that you are capable of some amazing things. You'll be amazed to discover what you can endure and what you're actually capable of. Don't let your disability or physical limitation define you. When you succeed in your business, those limitations become irrelevant.

## Take Action

The process for overcoming your unique disability is the same as for most barriers. Separate your belief barrier from the actual barrier. Look for staff or technology to help you bypass your barrier and lean into business models that don't require that which you lack.

## PRACTICAL BARRIER #3 - I'M DEAF OR HAVE A SPEECH IMPEDIMENT

If this is your situation, you have to focus more on text and visual elements. You can write books or articles, and no one will ever even know you are deaf. I write by dictation to deal with the problem of my eyes, but if your limitation is with your ears, you have to go in the opposite direction. Lean towards visual and creative arts.

If you have a speech impediment, you have to remember that adults don't really care. I have quite a few friends with speech impediments. One of my friends is deaf in one ear, so he speaks with his mouth to the left. I rarely notice it, and I really don't care.

I have another friend with a strong and significant stutter. I didn't notice it for more than six months. I just don't care about how he speaks nearly as much as I care about what he has to say. By the time I noticed his stutter, we'd been friends for a really long time. I always thought that was just the way he talked. It's never crossed my mind to make fun of an adult who has a speech impediment.

As adults, we don't think these things are big deals. We're too busy thinking about ourselves. We're such narcissists that we don't care about other people's impediments. The beauty of the online world is that even if you record a bunch of training videos, and they're filled with stuttering, you can clip out those stutters, so the final version sounds amazing. All your stuttering can be digitally removed.

**Take Action**

Focus on business models that don't require you to speak. If you're listening to the audio version of this book, you're not hearing my voice. I have someone else read each of my audiobooks because it's outside my skill set. You probably wouldn't have noticed if I didn't tell you.

There is a way around every single barrier.

## PRACTICAL BARRIER #4 - I'M DYSLEXIC

If you have a medical condition that inhibits your ability to read or write correctly, you can choose to see it as a hurdle that you can overcome rather than a limitation. It's simply an obstacle that you have to jump over.

Instead of writing, you can focus on audio and video content. You can hire an editor. You can do everything you want to do, but just use technology or a person to clean up what you've written. You can use the exact same process as people whose second language is English.

If you are worried about your readers being put off by typos, you can explain in the introduction of every single book, "I apologize if there are any grammatical or spelling mistakes in this book. I'm dyslexic. I hired an editor, and I use software to bridge the gap, but sometimes my mistakes slip through. If you notice one of those mistakes, please visit my typo page. You can flag it out, and I will fix it."

If you are open about it, you'll find that no one is mean to you. People give you more grace, and your audience will help you overcome your challenges.

My audience still submits typos to me so that I can

continue to tweak and improve my books. Even after they've been through multiple professional editing processes, a sentence occasionally slips through the crack, or there's an extra "s" that shouldn't be there. These things happen. Sometimes, it takes several people to read the same sentence before one notices that there's a mistake.

Whatever your limitation is, you can overcome it. Don't see it as a barrier, but simply as a characteristic as irrelevant as having blue or brown eyes. It's not something that affects your ability to generate revenue, take care of your family, and build a successful online business.

## Take Action

If you skipped straight to this particular barrier, you may have missed the consistent theme to overcoming barriers. It's very simple. Separate what you actually can't do from what you *think* you can't do. Find a way to bridge that barrier with software or an employee. And finally, lean into business models that focus on your area of strength rather than your weakness.

## PRACTICAL BARRIER #5 - STAGE FRIGHT

This is a very common type of fear. It affects a lot of people and in many different ways, ranging from traditional stage fright to social anxiety. Some people are afraid of speaking to people one-on-one, and going into a job interview can be their greatest nightmare.

I wrote several books on dealing with social anxiety and the fear of public speaking, but you can also decide to build a business where you don't have to face your fears. I don't ever have to get in front of a large audience and speak to them. It is not necessary for the growth of my business. Everything I do is online.

I do podcast episodes, but I record those when I'm by myself. I record Facebook live videos, but my audience is not in the room with me. I can't hear if they're saying bad stuff.

There's nothing to be afraid of. Technology has over-come that hurdle for us. Just build a business that works around your hurdle. You can use a drawing of yourself or a picture of someone else that's your avatar to fill in the gaps so that you don't have to be shy about the things that make you nervous. Over time, the things you're afraid of will diminish.

Every single hurdle that you think of as a reason why you can't succeed online can be overcome, and someone else has overcome it successfully. There are plenty of people making a killing online who can't do the math, spent some time in jail, never graduated from high school, or grew up in an unfortunate country. They had the deck dealt against them, but they turned things around in their favor. Each of these people puts proof to my one statement: "Each of these limitations is something you can overcome."

**Take Action**

The only way to overcome your fear of public speaking is to face it head-on. You can build a business that bypasses that need, or you can grab the bull by the horns. If you are really limited by the fear of public speaking, and you dread possible embarrassment, grab one of my books on social anxiety. It's a larger problem than a single activity can solve, and my other books walk you through overcoming this hurdle in a carefully paced and methodical manner.

# PRACTICAL BARRIERS REFLECTION QUESTIONS

1. Has your practical limitation held you back in life so far?
2. Has your barrier kept you from engaging with this book?
3. How much of your limitation comes from beliefs about your limitation rather than the limitation itself?
4. When was the last time you looked at the state of technology for your barrier?
5. What business models will work for someone with your unique limitation?
6. Are you ready to break through and stop letting your limitation define you?

# PRACTICAL BARRIERS ACTIVITY

It's time to become a breakthrough expert. My physical limitation with my eyes is very specific, and I could talk about it for days. Computer screens hurt my eyes. If I work too long on a traditional screen, my eyes will hurt so bad that I have to wear a blindfold for days. I'm completely incapable of working when this happens.

I can't be near other people's cell phones at night. I can feel the screen burning through my retinas and tearing my vision apart. At first, I dealt with my problem by visiting different types of doctors around the world. None of them offered me help or a solution.

I could write an entire book about my journey alone, but let's focus on the good part. Once I dialed into my exact limitation, I found ways around it. I switched my book writing entirely to dictation. It wasn't a choice for me; it was a necessity.

I have custom computer monitors with massive anti-blue light filters. Right now, I keep about 70 percent of the blue light blocked by the monitors. That's the maximum setting. On top of that, I have a software tool that keeps my computers in a perpetual night mode, pushing down that painful blue light even more. I keep the backgrounds on my monitors black and often, when I visit websites, I use a plugin that changes them to a grey background.

I do a great deal of work, including editing this book, using an e-ink tablet. It's quite expensive and nowhere near as fast or powerful as my wife's iPad; however, it doesn't burn my eyes to look at. Ereader screens don't hurt my eyes at all.

And that leads directly to your activity. You should be an expert on every single tool and piece of technology you can use to bypass your limitation. I know about every single ereader the second it's announced. I follow multiple ereader blogs and carefully keep my eyes on the technology. I have high hopes that full-color screens with fast enough refresh rates will enter the market within the next few years.

I could talk about this subject for hours, and you should have the same level of knowledge. Right now I'm able to work using my special computer monitors for a few hours per day, but there is no guarantee that solution will last. If my vision ever collapses to the next level, I'm ready to switch to using my special tools full-time. And if my vision goes further, I have an amazing team in place to support me and help me keep my books coming.

# 38

# RING OF EARTH MASTERY

LEAVE YOUR BARRIERS BEHIND

In my other books, I often talk about my lack of faith in psychology. I just don't believe that talking about negative things over and over again leads to a solution. How many times have married couples entered counseling only to be advised to list their grievances against the other person? As though hearing every negative thought a person has ever had about you will lead you to fall back in love with them.

In the same way, I don't want to focus on the negative. We've now broken through the hardest part of this book. Making it this far separates you from the pack, and I'm very excited to bring you into the final three Rings. This is where the magic happens. Take a moment to reset your mind and leave the negativity behind.

We had to fight our way through the swamp, and some of us might have had to leave some baggage back there. It's okay because now you are one step closer to the light. From here on out, we are moving from the emotional to the practical. The steps of this process will become far more literal and require less creative thinking.

We are going to follow a series of very specific steps to unlock the brilliance that lies within you. I'm excited to join you in the next Ring.

# ELEMENT THREE WATER – ASSETS

# 39

# THE SHAPE OF WATER

D on't get set into one form, adapt it and build your own, and let it grow, be like water.
- Bruce Lee[1]

IT SHOULD COME as no surprise that I'm a massive Bruce Lee fan. Similar to Musashi, he accomplished many great things in his short life, and the peak of his brilliance was the martial art he created, Jeet Kune Do. While translated literally as "the way of the intercepting fist," this martial art was the first one to realize that different people have different bodies.

The core principle is to fight with the body you have rather than the body you wish you had. As someone who's always had the look of a non-athlete, this resonated with me. And by the end of this Ring, it will resonate with you.

John Daly is often known as the most unexpected of successful golfers. He's overweight, smokes and drinks far too much. Yet he continues to succeed on the golf course.

Recently, when he lost a significant amount of weight, he discovered that his putting was actually worse.[2]

He had learned to play golf with one body type, and changing his body forced him to change the way he played. He had to retrain himself to use his new, healthier body.

Water is often considered to be the weakest of the elements, but that couldn't be further from the truth. Water can quickly change its form, from ice to steam. And each form is powerful in its own way. Rain pours onto the road in front of your house and seems powerful. But add a little cold, and tiny bits of water turn to ice in the road. They expand and eventually crack the road into pot holes. That which we build, water has the power to destroy.

Water made the grand canyon, and that should inspire you.

In this Ring, we delve into what makes you powerful. Each person who reads this book will come away with a different set of results. Each of us has a unique mix of strengths. Whatever form your water takes, know that we will use it to make you unstoppable.

Most of us don't know our worth and spend our lives conforming to other people's expectations of us. We let our boss determine our worth. We are controlled by far too many external forces.

In this Ring, we will assess your entire value, but that's just the starting place. This Ring is also about turning malleable water into firm ice.

We need a place of strength and a foundation from which to build your business. That power comes from knowing who you are. Most of us have accomplishments, skills, and resources that we have forgotten about.

In the Ring of Water, we are going to sort and sift everything. The greatest assets will rise to the top, and we will focus on your development strategically.

As you work your way through the Ring of Water, keep in mind one core question: which of these skills, assets, or resources can I leverage into profit the fastest?

In the Fourth Ring, we are going to combine Flame with Water to create fast and potent profit.

# 40

# YOU'RE WORTH MORE THAN YOU THINK

This is my absolute favorite part of this process. Instead of talking about the things that have held you back for far too long, we get to talk about the things that make you awesome. Every single week, people email me copies of their assessments asking for feedback, and I get so excited. I love focusing on what makes you great.

When it comes to self-assessment, most of us are terrible. We're not good at assessing our value, our worth, and what we bring to the table. This is why, in most negotiations, people who are untrained or inexperienced will dramatically undervalue their service.

You're worth more than you think. The first thing I did when my wife and I bought this hostel was give everyone working there a raise. They resisted at first. They came from a previous regime and felt that they were worth their previous wage.

I had to say, "I'm sorry. You can either take the raise or you're fired. I cannot look myself in the mirror knowing I underpay you. It will haunt me for the rest of my life. It's not about you; it's about me."

But it's *your* job to determine what your worth is. That's a big part of the purpose of this book. In the last section, we focused on the barriers that have been holding you back for far too long. Now, instead of fighting against the negative, we want to move into the positive.

Assessing your worth comes down to looking at the totality of your value as a person. Besides assessing your gear, it means looking at your skills and talents, relationships, passion, runway, and drive. Let me take you through each of these, so you can get a deep understanding of how important you are.

# 41

# DON'T HIDE YOUR LIGHT UNDER A BUSHEL

As you're assessing yourself, you need to understand and value your worth. Don't hide your worth under a bushel. We are so afraid of coming off as prideful or arrogant that we tend to mask our accomplishments.

When we overvalue our worth, we price ourselves out of the market. We put such a high value on our time that nobody can afford it. As long as you aren't the most expensive person in the world, don't worry about accidentally overvaluing yourself. Sometimes, people have so much pride that they massively inflate the price of their business, and I see this all the time on investment shows.

We are afraid of that mistake, so we pull too far in the other direction. When you're just getting started out, it's most likely that you will undervalue your skills, assets, and resources. Fortunately, you are not alone! When in doubt, please ask for feedback from your fellow Tribe Members in the Facebook group or email me. I'll be happy to provide an objective reality check if you are in the 1 percent of people overvaluing rather than undervaluing their worth.

For now, let's focus on the rest of us. It is far more common for you to undervalue your abilities. People who do this generate a glass ceiling that blocks them from achieving greatness. Undervaluing yourself can block far more than your entrepreneurial aspirations. Do any of these sound familiar?

- I'd love to do that job, but I'm not good enough.
- I shouldn't take the honors program because I'm not smart enough. I won't do well in that program.
- I wont apply because they are just going to hire someone else.
- They offered me the job because they feel bad for me.
- I only got this opportunity because of who my parents are.

My wife and I are currently trying to hire a manager for our small hotel, but we can't seem to find anyone who's the right fit for this job. Many people apply and say, "I just want to be a cleaner; I don't really want to be a manager."

The manager role pays twice as much, and it's half the work. All they have to do is arrange trips, talk the guests into going on them and then join them and have a good time. I'm amazed that there aren't more people clamoring for this job.

Many of our applicants think they're not good enough. They don't believe in themselves. They undervalue their ability, and they're not willing to fight through that glass ceiling. We also see this tendency in people who don't think they're smart enough or good enough to build their own business, or who think what they know how to do isn't valuable.

As you start to master the Ring of Water, let go of any preconceptions about how people will perceive you. An honest assessment is not a sign of arrogance. Only accuracy will bring you to the life you deserve.

## ASSET ONE - SKILLS

Skills and talents are not the same thing. A talent is an ability you are born with, but a skill is something you can improve. You can learn to program websites, speak better English, or do excellent work with spreadsheets.

Everybody in the world can sing. We are all somewhere on the spectrum of terrible to amazing. The way you sing without lessons is a talent. However, there is an element to singing that is a skill. You can improve your ability to sing with training.

I am not a good singer, and I am aware of this. Twice in my life people have taken me aside to let me know that I'm a terrible singer. Each time, they were worried that they would shatter my dreams. Fortunately, self-assessment is about analyzing your strengths honestly. With training, I have improved from a terrible singer all the way up to being a bad singer. Now, you can listen to my singing without the need to plug your ears or throw yourself out of a window to escape the sound of my voice.

This is not to say that I have low self-confidence when it

comes to singing. I'm simply able to assess the level of my talent.[1]

Most of what you think is a talent is actually a skill. I am not a talented writer. Most writers are more talented than me. But I don't see writing as a talent. I see it as a skill that I am constantly improving.

I look at things I wrote six or seven years ago, and I'm shocked. I've grown so much. Writing is the centerpiece of my life. It's my passion. I love doing it. I'm trying to create a business where I can write every day. That's my dream. I would love to spend three or four hours every single day dictating for the rest of my life. Ideally, for more than sixty years. I'd like to live a nice long life.

People often read my books and think I was born with a typewriter in front of me. The truth is I didn't write anything of consequence until I was thirty. I've always been fascinated and passionate about the different arts, and even though I've never been great at writing, I found a way to develop this skill.

## Skills Matter

I first discovered the value in skills when I was in college. I had one friend who was a barber. He thought his skill was worthless, so, he didn't want me to tell anyone. I said, "What are you talking about? Everyone needs haircuts all the time."

I remember the look in his eyes as he told me that he felt this ability was worthless. Because he believed it was worthless, his career fizzled – not through lack of ability, but through lack of faith in its worth.

Because he believed something had no value, it had no value. There's nothing I hate more than people who have greatness and throw it away through lack of belief. It's a self-fulfilling prophecy, and it drives me crazy.

I received an email last year from a reader who said, "Jonathan, your book is amazing. It so inspired me. I've always wanted to write fiction. I was in the military, forward-deployed for more than twenty years. I can't tell you exactly where because I was often operating in countries we're not allowed to talk about. When that career finished, I worked in espionage for twenty years. Do you think I could write a fiction story people would be interested in?"

I was so astounded I didn't know how to respond. His life sounded amazing. All I could think about was *The Bourne Identity* and every other book and movie that I love. His core area of expertise was the area that many people around the world find fascinating and irresistible.

While people not believing in themselves breaks my heart, when I can help them realize their greatness and do something amazing that customers want, that's the greatest feeling for me. That's where my great joy comes from.

As you're assessing yourself, write down every skill you have and what your level is for each. It's very simple. Take out your Breakthrough Journal and write down everything you've learned since you were a child and how good you are at each thing. You might have skills you haven't thought about in a long time.

Older skills often circle back and become important after a time where they faded away. We went through a period where typing was really important and taught in schools on typewriters. Then, as we transitioned to computers, the skill faded away for a while. I never learned typing in school.

I was educated in the period in between learning to type

on a typewriter and a computer. I had to teach myself to type fast in high school because it was holding me back.

As more and more people communicate via phones and tablets, the ability to type fast is diminishing again with this generation. They are going to have to relearn that skill.

As you look back at your skills, write everything down, even if it is decades old. When I'm practicing my copywriting, I often study ads from the 1880s and find many skills that are powerful and still valuable today.

In addition to writing down each skill you possess, keep track of how quickly you can accelerate that skill into something you could sell. If you have some ability with graphic design, how much training until you could sell your designs to clients? Any skill that you could learn quickly should be added to this list.

## Take Action

All of the Ring of Water is an activity. Write down your answers for each of these sections in your Breakthrough Journal. The more creative you get with this section, the more powerful it can be. I like to outline projects in multiple colors. It makes the work a little jauntier, and I find it's more effective for me.

Do whatever it takes to make your Water Ring effective.

## ASSET TWO - TALENTS

Talents are your innate abilities. These are things where you naturally shine and could be things that you've taken for granted for a long time. People who are good-looking often forget that not everyone gets treated as nicely as they do. If you're handsome, make sure to write that down.

Perfect pitch is the best example of a talent you either have or you don't.

Any area where you have an edge goes into this category. It's okay to mix in talents with skills. We can often improve our talents with training.

The important part of this process is to come up with a master list of the things you are good at. Mixing up the definition of talents and skills doesn't matter as long as you create a complete list.


**Take Action**

Write down a list of all your natural abilities, talents, and advantages. Do you have:

- A really good memory?
- Perfect pitch?
- Natural instincts when it comes to color or design?
- Extremely flexible ankles?

Write down anything that makes you stand out from the crowd and remember this core principle: skills can improve talents.

By the end of this exercise, you should have a pretty long list of things you are good at.

## ASSET THREE - EXPERTISE

In addition to skills and talents, there is also a lifetime of accumulated knowledge. Expertise will determine the business you build, while skills and talents will determine how you build it.

I have a great deal of expertise when it comes to writing non-fiction. I've written over 200 successful books and feel confident in my experience. I have improved over the past decade, and I have a system I follow to write every one of my books.

I could take that expertise and leverage it in a host of ways. I could share my expertise through in-person coaching, online videos, books or audio training. The content comes from my expertise, but the transmission modality will come from your skills and talents.

No matter how much I would like to, I can't teach via singing. I lack the necessary talent.

Take a moment to assess your knowledge. Are you a master at fantasy football? Can you name every sneaker produced in the past twenty years? Do you know everything about mattresses?

## Take Action

Create a master list of your areas of expertise. Whether you love reading books about World War II, or you have been working in the same industry for forty years, it goes on the list.

As you begin to build new revenue streams, we will leverage your existing expertise as much as possible.

# ASSET FOUR - GEAR

Every teenage band has a member who got invited because he has a van. The right gear can make up for a lack of talent in many areas. When you're starting a band, whoever owns a set of drums or a van is going to get invited automatically. Plenty of people own guitars, but drums are a rarer commodity. They are big, bulky, and expensive.

Go through your attic and basement. Find old costumes and pieces of electronics that you haven't thought about in years. It's better to err on the side of a list that is too comprehensive, rather than one that is lacking. Some of the craziest and most successful businesses started with the simplest of gear.

There used to be a YouTube channel my kids watched relentlessly. Videos of adults wearing superhero costumes and being silly to public domain music.[1] I was shocked the first time I realized my daughter was watching a video with over a billion views. There was nothing special about the music or the costumes, which had clearly come from low-end Halloween shops. They were not fancy, and they clearly didn't need to be.

I have accumulated a lot of gear over the eight years of my career. I have loads of old cameras and video cameras that we no longer use. I do 90 percent of my work using the camera on my phone these days. But that doesn't mean that gear doesn't work. It's still awesome, and if I need to do a multi-camera[2] setup, I can.

I bet you have equipment left over from past hobbies or things your kids tried and gave up on. Crazy costumes can be leveraged into some surprising successes. If you don't know you have it, you won't come up with great ways to use it. So document all your gear.

Price and newness aren't nearly as important here. I replace my laptop every three to four years, and that's only because I do a lot of work with video. If I didn't record and edit my own videos, I could keep using my laptop from 2010. Most of the flashy features on new computers don't matter unless you're playing new video games or editing video. Even photography doesn't require high-end equipment anymore.

## Take Action

Continue to build a list of your assets and now include all the equipment that you own. You will find that you have to keep adding to this list as you find uses for stuff you never thought was useful.

When I first started recording live videos nearly a decade ago, I used a three-by-three-meter piece of dark felt as my background. I didn't have anything to hang it from, so I duct-taped my background to the wall for each recording. Then I had to take it down. That old, useless piece of cloth might not be so useless anymore!

## ASSET FIVE - RELATIONSHIPS

Friends are an asset. It's amazing what people will share with if you treat them and their stuff with respect. You can gain access to people's talents, skills, and resources because of your network, but you can also lose it all if you don't treat it with respect.

When I loan things out to people, and they don't return it in the way they received it, they never get to touch my stuff again. This is how everyone is. I have loads of cameras, video cameras, wires, and microphones that I've collected over my career. Our staff at the hotel gets access to all these tools. We have multiple waterproof cameras because we're always taking pictures of our kids in the water. We are happy to let people on our team use those things as long as they don't break them.

As you look at your relationships, make a list of the skills, talents, and resources that these get you access to. Perhaps one of your friends is an expert at a skill you'd love to master, and they can mentor you. Perhaps they have the ability to introduce you to people who have the asset you're looking for. Assessing relationships is not just about getting access to their stuff but also their knowledge and networks.

Do you have a friend who could introduce you to someone who's talented or who's doing what you want to be doing? There's a reason I have so many courses and books on networking. It's the foundation of all business. It is not what you know; it's who you know.

No matter who you are, you have friends and acquaintances and therefore potential access to things that are interesting and can bring value to your business.

## Take Action

When creating a relationship list, you might find it easier to work in a circle with a mind map. The center of the circle is you, and the first layer is your closest friends, relatives, and family members. Next to each of these close contacts, make a master list of their skills, talents and gear. A lot of people have old gear that they don't use anymore but would be awesome for you. It's worth talking to each of these people because who knows what might be waiting for you in their garage?

Speaking of garages, maybe a friend has some empty space you can use while you're getting started.

Each circle out from the center will be filled with people you have a weaker connection with. You might need to create three or four circles outside your closest friends as you build out your network assessment. Your family members will be near the center, and the acquaintance you met once or twice will be in the outermost ring.

The rings are about more than just how well you know someone; they are also a visualization of the strength of the relationship. And that translates into how likely they are to share assets and resources with you.

Make a master list of everything you can think of, from gear to connections.

I used to use my friend's studio at night. They had an amazing recording studio because one of my friends is an unbelievable musician. She would record music during the day, but her studio was always closed after 10:00 PM.

She gave me free reign from 10PM to 6AM. As long as the studio looked like I'd never been there, I was allowed to do whatever I wanted. I just had to leave it the way I found it. They had an amazing green screen setup that I used to record a lot of my early videos and shoot a lot of my early pictures when I began building my business.

# ASSET SIX - PASSION

Passion is the fuel that will keep your business going when things get tough. I still have bad days and days where I feel like procrastinating. Some days, I just want to take the kids to the beach for the whole day. If I didn't love my work, it would be hard to keep building this business.

A critical metric is *desire*. The more passion you have for a business, the more likely it is to succeed. When things get tough, and the desire to quit rears its ugly head, it's a lot easier to stick with a business you love than a job you're struggling to get excited about.

When we're looking at different business models and what you bring to the table, how much do you enjoy doing it? If you have an amazing video camera setup, but you hate video cameras, you've got a dichotomy there. You have to go one way or the other. I don't want you to build a business doing something you hate.

One of the guys I work with loves writing books, but he would rather die than make a video product because he's obsessed with his privacy. Even when I said, "Well, you can make a slideshow video, never show your face, and you can

even pay someone else to read the content for the videos."
He said, "No, I still don't want to do it."

You can't force someone to do something they are not
comfortable with. As you look at each of these different
skills, assets, and expertise, look at how passionate you are
about them. That's how we assess how useful they are. You
want to find out what you're really excited about.

Hands down, my favorite part of the business is
outlining books. I know it sounds crazy, but the only thing I
like more than writing is outlining. That's why I have over
one hundred books outlined in my notebook, yet, I've only
written a few dozens in the last year.

As you're working through this list, think of the skills
you are excited about and you can learn or acquire quickly.
Sometimes, there are skills you are a short distance away
from mastering. If you're good at one thing with math, grab-
bing another math skill isn't that hard. If you love audio
engineering, learning video engineering isn't a huge jump.

Look at your relationships again and see if there are
things that they know and you'd love to learn about. Can
they help you or advise you in any way?

## Take Action

With your master list of skills, talents, and gear, we want to
add a final layer. Rank your desires on a scale of 1-10.

How much does the thought of focusing on that asset
make you feel? If you absolutely hate it, then write the
number zero. And if you love it, write the number ten.

Starting a business that you know you're going to hate is
no way to build a future, so we want to avoid that as much as
possible.

## ASSET SEVEN - RUNWAY

How much runway do you have available? This is how much time you have on the clock before you're in trouble. If you just quit your job, and you have enough money to keep your family going for six months, then you've got six months of runway.

We all come from different situations, and your runway might need a very different calculus. Maybe you have a family, and you can't quit your job because you need it to support them. But if every night, from 10 PM to midnight, you can put in two hours on your project after everyone's gone to sleep, you have two hours of runway per night. You just measure it in a different way.

I don't come from the start-up world. I was never able to say, "Hey, let's borrow a couple million dollars from some investor, burn it over the course of the next eighteen months, and hope that by the time we get to the end of the runway, we don't crash."

That's how Silicon Valley sees runway, but we have to plan it differently. There is no fiery explosion at the end of your runway. That's not my philosophy or business model.

Runway is simply how much time you've got before you need to start making things work. There are lots of ways you can extend that runway, which I'm going to teach you in the Ring of Flame. But you need to know how much runway you currently have before we determine what you need to do to extend it.

## Take Action

Assess your unique life situation. How can you measure runway? Is it in days, weeks, or months? Do you have to stick with your current career until you hit a specific financial goal? When you replace your current daily income with income from your new business, can you quit that old job and grow your runway?

Assess your finances, speak to your loved ones, and create a realistic runway plan. How much time and resources can you invest in your new venture? What targets do you have to hit to expand that runway?

Create a firm idea of the path in front of you.

## ASSET EIGHT - DRIVE

Drive is your engine. It is how hard and fast you will push. My drive has gone up and down throughout my career. Once I started having more kids, my drive got a lot more intense. It kicked into high gear. I'm not a fancy guy up on a cloud, living up on a mountain. I'm fighting to get what I need and to build my business. That's how much drive I have.

If you inherited a bunch of money, you might not have a lot of drive. You can tell the difference between a person who has worked for three summers to raise enough money to buy the worst car on the lot, but they own it and bought it with her own blood, sweat, and tears, and the person whose parents bought them a brand-new car when they were sixteen.

When I was in high school, one of the other kids had a DeLorean. He did not appreciate that car one iota. It was just a thing his parents had bought him. The lessons we learn and the amount of effort we have to put in to acquire things earlier affect our drive level later on in life.

Reflect on and assess how much drive you have. How willing are you to do whatever it takes?

Here's another way of measuring drive:

### How much adversity will it take to make you quit?

I faced a lot of adversity in this business. I thought I was going blind a year and a half ago, but quitting never crossed my mind. Instead, I thought, "How can I fight through this challenge and build a business that continues to grow? I don't have any interest in staying at the same level. I want to get bigger and help more people. I want more."

When challenge met my drive, my drive crushed it. Look at how much drive you have and be honest with yourself. How bad do you want to have your own business? How hard are you willing to work to secure your retirement or the future of your family?

I have something that I say to myself a lot: "Into every life, a little doo-doo must flow." Part of succeeding in any business is about looking in the mirror and saying exactly how much trash you're willing to eat to get where you need to go.

Several years ago, when I met the woman who would become my wife, I was coasting. I was making an unbelievable amount of money online, and I had enough to support myself for quite a while.

We got together, we fell in love, and we started having children. There came a moment where coasting wasn't working anymore. We didn't have enough money, and my drive went through the roof. I was still recovering from how much time I'd taken off and how much slacking I'd done. It was my own fault, and I knew it.

We needed money.

I took a job writing a book for a friend of mine – thirty-five thousand words for eight hundred dollars. Two weeks of work for a measly eight hundred bones was a big step back for someone who had made seven figures two years earlier. I could have said, "I'm too good for this job."

I could have let pride into the picture, but I looked at my kids and said to myself, "Sometimes, you got to eat a little crow."

Drive is what will get you through the dirt and the pain. I would love to promise you that building a new business is going to be unicorns and rainbows, but it's not. This book is about making you strong and powerful. It's about giving you the ability to overcome those tough moments. The more drive you have, the more powerful you are.

The beauty is that drive is a skill. You can get better at it. You can believe in yourself more. You can fight harder. You can put in longer hours, and you can get stronger. That's part of the training I'm going to introduce you to in the Ring of Flame.

As you work through your assessment, be honest with yourself. How much drive do you have? Would you take a crappy job from one of your friends to make ends meet so you can keep building your business? Or are you looking for any excuse to quit?

**Take Action**

Measure your drive and be honest with yourself. How much adversity before you quit? Have you started a business in the past and given up at the first hurdle? Will you quit if you don't make money in the first month? Or are you here to win?

Are you going to stick with this journey until you carve

out the life you deserve? Are you going to do whatever it takes to secure your future?

Would you take a crappy job from one of your friends to make ends meet so you can keep building your business? Or are you looking for any excuse to bail on this book and call me a liar?

Write down a clear statement of your drive in your Breakthrough Journal. I shared my drive statement at the start of this book, when I promised that if you bleed with me, I'll bleed with you. Now it's your turn to make the same commitment.

# 42

## FROM WATER TO ICE

You now have a pretty awesome list of things that make you unique, and you should treasure it. You are far more than the sum of your parts. In the Ring of Flame, we will begin to look at ways you can leverage your assets into fast profits.

I'm starting to get more excited, and I hope that you are too.

You can take your assets and focus on them until they are as strong as ice. You have the power to bring mountains to their knees and carve canyons into the earth. You are unstoppable; you just didn't realize it yet.

In case you need one more metaphor to get your blood pumping, I have one locked and loaded. People always think that water is weak and light. But when they pick up a bucket of water, they realize that it's quite heavy. The average bathtub in the United States holds about eighty gallons of water. When you slide in, the water feels weak.

A single gallon of water weighs 8.34 pounds. Eighty of those gallons fills a bathtub with 667.2 pounds. Good luck finding someone strong enough to lift that!

Just because people have underestimated you in the past, that does not mean you aren't powerful.

# RING OF WATER REFLECTION QUESTIONS

1. Are you surprised at some of the assets you came up with?
2. How many forgotten resources did you discover?
3. Do you feel like you bring more to the table now than you did when you started this chapter?
4. Does the thought of asking your friends for access to their resources make you feel nervous?
5. Are you excited to take these resources and convert them into a profitable business?
6. Where do your passion, expertise, and assets intersect?
7. If you could build any dream business based on your existing assets, what would it be?
8. Are you starting to notice the discrepancy between what your boss thinks you're worth and your true value?
9. Are you ready to get paid what you're actually worth?

# RING OF WATER MASTERY

There is a very good chance that your list is really messy now. You probably came up with loads of ideas throughout this chapter and had to go back and add them to your earlier list. Take that dirty list and make it into something organized and color coded.

Having a structure to your assets will make it easier for you to go through everything and find what you're looking for. An organized list will make you feel even more excited about the assets you bring to the table.

As you reorganize your list, try to rank each asset based on value and feasibility. Rank every skill, talent, and area of expertise on a scale of 1-10. If you have worked as a cameraman for ten years, then your camera handling score will be a 10. If you've never even seen a video camera, your expertise score is a zero. In the next column, add in your passion ranks. How much would you like to use this skill in building your next business? Does the thought of focusing on this niche fill you with joy or dread?

Look for ways you can combine different assets. You can

combine your video cameras with a friend who edits videos to turbocharge that asset.

You might find it easier to circle your biggest areas of passion in green and cross out the ones you hate in red. Get as visual and artistic as you need!

As we build a business model, we want to find a place where your ability, desire, and profitability intersect.

# ELEMENT FOUR FLAME – FAST MONEY

# 45

## THE UNQUENCHABLE FLAME

In college, I was a volunteer on an ambulance for a year. A single semester of training, and I was qualified as an EMT-B. I have plenty of stories that still haunt me nearly two decades later, and I don't often talk about the things that I saw during that time. But there is one story I can share with you.

One night, my crew and I stopped for dinner at a fast food restaurant. We parked in between the restaurant and the furniture store next door. As I was stepping out of the ambulance, a cigarette arced from the road across the parking lot and landed in a tiny bush at the corner of the furniture store. Normally, nothing happens when a cigarette is flicked from a car window. But this night, the odds went the other way.

The bush caught on fire.

This was the first time I had ever seen a real fire in the wild. I had seen plenty of barbecues and fireplaces, but this was a different beast entirely. This was an untamed monster. Most people have no idea what a real fire is like.

Our ambulance carried two fire extinguishers, one on each side. While one of my squad mates grabbed the closer extinguisher, I rushed around the ambulance and grabbed the other one. In the few seconds it took me to walk around the ambulance, the fire had grown.

When I started my journey, it was a cute little fire, only a few inches tall. When I came back it was a raging inferno, scraping at the eaves of the furniture store more than ten feet in the air. I was shocked.

If we had arrived just thirty seconds later, that furniture store would have been destroyed. Fire is a fast and powerful force. And you are now going to harness that energy.

I know something about you that you hopefully isolated in the Water Ring: there is a time when your energy will run out, and you will give up. We all have a breaking point.

Thousands of people will read this book and get excited as they start. They will be filled with emotional energy and drive. But then they won't participate in a single activity. They will burn out too quickly because all they have is kindling.

I wrote a book called *20K a Day* that includes everything I know about writing fast and effectively. That book gets exactly two types of reviews: people who tried the activities and people who didn't. Writers give it a five-star review as they track their success, and that makes me feel very good.

Unfortunately, many people give the book a one-star review and complain that it's too long. They never say that the activities didn't work. I've never gotten a negative review like that. Their excitement burned out too fast. I'm sure they tell themselves that if the book had been shorter, they would have tried the exercises. (The new edition is half the length of the old, so we'll soon find out if that's true.)

That's sweet, but they are deluding themselves.

In the Flame Ring, we are going to add more fuel to the fire, so that your passion keeps burning long after you finish reading this book. You will stay the course and last long enough to achieve the success that I know resides within you.

## MINIMUM DISTANCE TO PROFIT

Now that we've talked about the barriers you can break through in the Earth Ring and your existing assets and skills in the Water Ring, we want to transform those into money as quickly as possible.

**The shorter the distance between now and the moment where you start to make money using the techniques, philosophies, and strategies from this book, the greater your odds of success.**

As much as we want to believe, like Dumbo holding onto that red feather, I need to get that first dollar into your hand as quickly as possible to make it real. It's all well and good to get excited by a book, but if you don't see results in a short enough period of time, your faith will wither and die. I don't want that to happen. I want to give you greatness.

The goal of the Ring of Flame is very simple - to make you money as fast as possible.

## GET PAID TO LEARN

The fastest way to minimize the distance between you and profit begins with our first technique: getting paid to learn. This is how I started my online business. I looked at the skills and assets I had. I knew that I had a basic understanding of certain markets, and I said to myself, "I could learn how to do SEO using software and training and tools quickly, but I can't afford the course I want."

I put an ad on Craigslist, "Local SEO expert looking for clients." I closed my first client that week. I asked for five hundred dollars, but she paid me two hundred. She handed me a check and I couldn't believe it. I used that to merely buy the software that I would use to rank both her website and mine. The next client gave me enough money to start buying the courses that I needed to learn and master the skill I was developing.

One of the best ways to learn how to become a copywriter is to get a low-paying job writing emails, ads, and sales letters and use that money to buy a training course to walk you through the process, so you can learn new skills and do a pretty good job at the same time. It's very effective.

What's beautiful about this process is that you get paid, and you're learning on someone else's dime. On top of that, your motivation comes from the fact that you have to do a good job because you cannot afford to pay a refund if the client is not satisfied. You have already spent their money.

This system has always worked for me. It's one of my favorite ways to begin building a business. To get started, look at which skill or asset you can leverage the fastest. Which of those could you generate income from the fastest? Which of those can you learn the fastest? Where do you have the smallest knowledge gap?

If you're already an expert at something, you might be able to sell coaching or consulting in that field. And it's not just your skills – it can also be your gear. I live on a tropical island where people come from all over the world to learn how to surf, and they all want to record a video of their first lesson. You can rent out your action video camera for a few weeks to cover the entire purchase price here.

There is no better way to invest in your company than to get others to pay for the training, software, and equipment you need.

## Take Action

Look at your existing assets. Look for skills that you would like to learn, could learn quickly, and that people would pay for you to learn. There are probably loads of online skills that you haven't even added to your list because you haven't considered them.

It's time to begin making a list of the skills you'll need to grow your business. Everything from web design to learning how to write a blog post is on the table. There is a good chance you will revisit this activity after reading the Void Ring, but begin the process now.

There are always skills you can learn for less than people will pay you to learn them. This is the first piece of low-hanging fruit.

# 48

## FAST VS SLOW MONEY

There are two ways you can make money online. The first is to get a little bit of money quickly, which I call fast money. The second is to get more money or a percentage of the action in the long term. This is slow money.

These are the two ways people can pay me for writing a sales letter for them. They can pay a set amount of money at the start of the project. They pay cash, I deliver the project, and my role in the project is done. The second way is for them to pay me a smaller amount up front, but I get a percentage of the sales.

This is a common practice in the copywriting world. The highest-level copywriters only get paid a percentage of the increase. If they take a product generating $50,000 a month and take it to $60,000 a month, they just get a percentage of that $10,000 a month increase. Their percentage is often as high as 50 percent, but they only get paid 50 percent of the increase.

Those are big numbers, but they come with a higher level of risk. I've worked on multiple projects where the person has done unethical things or simply made bad decisions. I've worked on projects where I was supposed to get paid a percentage, but the person never launched the finished project. Fifty percent of nothing isn't that great. That's the nature of slow money – high risk, high reward.

The purpose of fast money is to build runway. The main way I generate fast money in my business right now is through ghostwriting. I use the money from a high-ticket ghostwriting project to pay for ads, hire technical staff, and pay for designs, sub-writers, researchers, and editors that work not only on the client's project but also my solo projects.

Runway gives you time and money you can use to build the other parts of your business. Many of us don't have enough runway to start off focusing on slow money. I believe in building out your fast money revenue streams first and then using the time that money gives you to start working on slow money projects. Fast money pays for the runway, and slow money allows you to take flight.

The beauty of slow money is that you get paid multiple times for the same work.

Whichever business model you decide to follow – I'm going to teach you six powerful models in the Void Ring – you'll go through this dichotomy as you're building your business. Some people start with huge amounts of runway, but the majority of us have a little bit of debt or some family obligations and need to build more runway first.

It reminds me of a little track toy I used to have from He-Man. The toy would drive along the track about eight inches, and then the track would rotate in front of the toy. It would then drive along the track again. This rotating piece of train track would keep flipping in front of the toy. Even though it had eight inches of track in front of it, it always had enough to continue going. You can continue to build your runway with fast money as your business gets closer to taking flight.

## Take Action

How much runway do you need to build? Do you need more money or more time to work on your projects? Most new entrepreneurs need to generate enough fast money to quit their day jobs and start focusing on their long-term vision. If you have already retired, you may have loads of time but very limited funding, so you will spend time until your fast money projects generate enough money for your slow money projects.

Which asset can you leverage into money the fastest? Do you have a space or equipment you can rent out? Can you start out recording voice-overs for books? Can you start doing the same thing you do at work as a freelancer to generate additional revenue?

Spend some time with your Breakthrough Journal and try to come up with as many creative ideas as you can before moving on to the next section.

# 49

## BET ON YOURSELF

There are two resources that we will use to build your new business: time and money. Whichever resource you have in more abundance, you will use to build your empire.

I still go back and forth in my business when I decide to invest in different parts of a project. Sometimes, I get excited by something I want to release quickly, and I'll design the graphics myself rather than using my full-time graphics team because I don't want to wait two or three days. That's me using time.

When building your business, look at what your time is worth and how much money you have available. If you have no money, use your time. If you have lots of money, be cautious. My experience is that people who enter this business with a great deal of money tend to be very inefficient in how they invest it.

A few years ago, I was at a conference for seven-figure marketers. I was shocked at all of these men wearing power ties. I thought, "Isn't the point of being an entrepreneur that you don't have to wear a power tie anymore, at least? You don't have to wear a hoodie and sneakers, but can't you at least unbutton that collar?"

I was speaking to one of these men, who clearly came from a great deal of money. He's what I call a dream client. High money, low reality. I asked him, "What do you pay for a squeeze page?" And he said, "Well, of course $25,000." At the time, the most expensive person in the entire country that I knew of was charging $3,000. He was so high up the mountain, he didn't even know what things actually cost. I feel like he was in charge of buying hammers for NASA in a previous life.

On the other hand, when we don't have money, we find ways to make it work anyways. It creates a different sense of urgency within us. Even if you have a lot of financial runway, I recommend that you focus on efficiency.

In order to grow your business and bet on yourself, you have to believe in yourself and your ability to bring a task to completion. This can be in small and big things. It begins by taking a job you don't know how to do and using that money to pay for the course, software, or training you need to learn that ability. That's risky – talk about betting on yourself.

When I say bet on yourself, I'm talking small money. I believe that you can succeed with what you have in front of you. What I design, sell, and provide through my training is a blueprint that works. I teach a business model that I've used in multiple markets, from writing books in different genres to providing training in different industries. If you follow the steps in the correct order, you will achieve success.

I have amazing people as part of my Facebook group

who have wonderful stories. They're passionate about things I don't even understand, ranging from haunted houses to voice-overs. I have two followers who are obsessed with mulch. I don't understand it in the slightest, but they get so excited talking about different types of beetles and ways to make the perfect mulch. No matter their passion, my followers find success as they follow the process.

But you have to believe that you deserve success. I believe you deserve it. Unfortunately, we often self-sabotage because there's a part of us that thinks we're unworthy. The Earth Ring is the largest part of this book, not because it's my favorite topic, but because I know that's where the majority of people get stuck – in the mud and quicksand. We all have that one special reason why *Breakthrough* will work for everyone except us.

If you don't believe you deserve success, you will always self-sabotage. No one else is going to hand you your dream job. No one else is going to make things go your way. I don't believe in luck and I don't believe in serendipity. I believe in getting your hands dirty and fighting for what you deserve, building products you believe in, building a business that you're proud of, and generating revenue that can support your family.

## Take Action

Take a long, hard look in the mirror. Do you believe that you deserve success and have what it takes to cross the finish line? The stronger your belief, the more emotional runway you will have available.

Even though you are "only" investing time, that is a very precious resource. If you don't believe you have what it takes to succeed, you will stop investing too soon.

Reaffirm your commitment to invest your time in this process and give yourself enough runway to achieve success. Make a decision to bet on the one person you know you can trust.

# 50

# EATING CROW

E ating crow is an unfortunate but real part of growing your business. Pride cometh before a fall. I have done some things in my business that I'm not proud of.

I am not proud of going to one of my friends and saying, "I will do any task you have available. I've got to pay a medical bill. I'll write you a sales letter. I'll create a video for you. I'll write a book for you, half price, whatever it takes." But sometimes, you have to choose between pride and sacrifice.

The country where I live has a fascinating real estate market. People believe in "buy and hold" here. Someone will buy a piece of real estate or build a house, decide what the house is worth, and say "This is the price." They will leave that house unsold and empty for decades to get that price.

I've seen situations where someone built the house, then died twenty years later, and their children are still trying to sell it because nobody is willing to pay the amount of money they want.

If they had accepted a lower amount of money, they could have sold the house within six months, built another one, sold it again, built another one, and sold it again. Over the course of those twenty years, they would have made ten or one hundred times more money. Pride held them back.

When you're deciding how to price things, you can say, "This is what it's worth, and I will wait as long as it takes. I will let my family starve. I will lose my home until someone offers me what it's worth."

Or you can say, "I'll take the low-paying gig to bridge the gap."

There is a balance, and that balance is different for everyone.

If you eat too much crow, you can get trapped and become stuck at that level. On the other hand, I know people in my business who will never lower their prices because they believe that if you sell something low-priced, you can never sell something high-priced. I don't believe that.

I like to create products that are available to everyone. My lowest-priced product is $7, and my most expensive costs more than $3,000. I don't write books for eight hundred bucks anymore. But if one of my kids gets sick, I'll do what-ever it takes. I'll eat that pie of crow. I won't do it with a smile on my face, but I'll do it.

Knowledge is knowing that sometimes you have to lower your price to make ends meet. Wisdom is knowing *when* to do it.

That comes from experience. The trade-off is that if you take a low-paying job that fills up your time, you don't have enough time to find other high-paying jobs. It's not that people perceive you at a particular price, it's that you lose the time to spend seeking those clients that would pay you a better amount.

You have to find your balance. You don't have to eat crow all the time. Just be willing to do it if you have to. Sometimes, you have to take a bad job to raise enough money to pay for the good job.

When you take low-paying jobs, you can lose a great deal of time, so I recommend you at least find low-paying jobs with low-maintenance clients. Some clients who pay the least will try to eat up all of your time. You don't want to work with someone who acts like they spent the last of their money with you. That becomes a nightmare.

With each job, assess how much money you will make and whether the project will shrink or grow your runway.

Don't get trapped in low-paying jobs that leave you no time to find the high-paying jobs you deserve. Crow is only used for bridging gaps when your back is against the wall.

**Take Action**

Most likely, you are going to start out massively undervaluing your work. This is what nearly everyone does, so it's unlikely you'll have to eat any crow in the short term. I just want to prepare you for that possibility when it comes calling a few months or years down the line.

Crack open your Breakthrough Journal and take a moment to look through your past. Have there been times in the past where you refused to budge on a fee and later realized you'd made a mistake? If you could go back and take the lower price, would you do it?

Have you taken jobs where you were underpaid and felt stuck working on a task you hated? Do you have past projects you regret working on?

Write down the situation and what you would say if you had a time machine and could whisper a piece of wisdom to this past version of you.

# 51

# THE EXPERTISE PERCEPTION

People pay experts more than they pay amateurs and they pay specialists more than generalists.

The expertise perception is the fulcrum you will use to raise your rates. When you're working on fast money, you can raise your rates much quicker than you realize. We often come to this mistaken belief that we're trapped – that once we agree on a rate with someone, that's our price forever. You can change your prices, and people won't care.

I had a friend who was a used-car salesman. He told me that a good deal was one where both people walked away happy.

That's the only metric that matters for your clients.

In our hostel, we are still figuring things out. We have a room that I priced too high and nobody booked it for a week. We lowered the price by a single dollar, and it's been full ever since. The change was tiny, but it made a real difference.

We have only one room with an air conditioner. When we first took over the hostel, the previous owners would rent out this room for far less than it was worth. We decided to shut that down, as the price was far too low. We turned it into our kids' room.

One day, I talked to my wife about putting the room back on the market. I said to her, "What price could we charge for that room that's worth the inconvenience of moving all our kids' stuff into our room for the night?"

Initially, she suggested doubling the previous price, but that was what she thought people would pay, not the price of our inconvenience. We decided to multiply the price by 2.5 and see what happened. Unfortunately, we underestimated demand. The room was rented out so often that we had to rent a second house for our kids to live in. The room is only empty a few nights a month right now.

We raised the price again this weekend to triple the old price. Less than a day later, someone rented it for two full weeks. They have no idea what the previous people paid, and they don't care. It doesn't even cross their minds. They saw that our best room was available, looked at the price, and decided the room was worth it.

You can and should raise your price between every single client. Double your price with each client, so that even if they talk you down, you still make more than you did on the last project.

Getting paid more is primarily about positioning. There are two ways to approach fast money. The first is to chase jobs. The perfect example of this is joining a website for outsourcers, such as UpWork. These are places where someone is hiring, posts a job, and then loads of people bid on it. You become a commodity.

I use UpWork to hire people all the time. Some of the people I've hired are brilliant. The guy I hired to write the script for the *Serve No Master* comic book is unbelievable. When I read what he wrote, I started crying. I finally understood how Alexander the Great felt when there were no more worlds left to conquer.[1]

He took my story and wrote in a way that I wish I could write. I dropped to my knees, and I had a long conversation with my editor where she talked me off the cliff. But the only thing more astounding than this man's level of talent was the pittance he charged me.

Loads of people were bidding on that project, including writers for the largest comic book companies in the world. Some of their resumes were unbelievable. When you're chasing jobs, and there are ten or twenty bids, prices go down. The bids were so low, it turned into a race to the bottom.

## When you have a competition for a job, the pricing is relative.

Instead of chasing jobs, you want to position yourself as an expert. This is what I teach with my methodology. This is why in the Ring of Void, I'll talk a great deal about establishing your presence online and building a website so that you engage in one-on-one conversations with potential clients.

I know people whose followings are significantly larger than mine, yet their revenue is much smaller. When you measure someone by the size of their email list, you often miss reality. My value is not on paper. I don't have a lot of followers. What I have is a lot of relationships.

Positioning is how I gain most of my clients. I tell everyone what I do, and I have a website demonstrating my expertise. If anyone says, "Hey, are you any good at launching books online?" All I have to do is point to about two years ago – actually the day I was having lunch with my publisher for this book, someone I've been friends with for almost a decade – my book was number two on Amazon. Book number three was *Harry Potter*. That put me on everyone's radar.

When you're an expert, people come to you. I have been cold-called by millionaires and even one billionaire who said he was shocked that I responded to his message. We worked on a project I'm very excited by, and that project came because of my positioning.

I simply tell people I'm an expert. If you want to be successful as a ghostwriter, act a little pretentious. It sounds crazy, but that's all it takes. When you're pretentious, people automatically assume you must be incredibly good and will pay whatever your rate is. That's positioning.

Turning down a bad job is scary. Sometimes you can't do it. But what I encourage you to do is to take jobs from low-maintenance clients when you have to eat crow. Try not to sell too much of your time. If you have to take a low-paying job, take it from someone who's going to email you once a month rather than someone who is going to call you three times a day.

Another way to extend your runway is to extend your project timeline. If you normally deliver a book in thirty days, when you take a lower-paying job, tell them you need ninety. This way, you have money coming in but also a little extra breathing room. Use that extra time to score clients that will pay what you're actually worth.

Positioning is about acting like an expert. At first, it's really hard to hide your inexperience. I know it seems like a catch-22, but we can break through this. If you act like an expert, people will treat you like one. In addition to doubling your price, act a little bit like a jerk. Don't be a complete monster, but increase how pretentious you behave by about 10 percent. This is a minor calibration, but it's enough to get people assuming you are great at your job. Nobody who is only average would be so full of themselves.

Here's how I get high-ticket ghostwriting clients. I tell everyone who asks that I'm a celebrity ghostwriter, and then I act like a snob. Not a total monster that people will hate, but someone who has enough clients that I can choose to work with. This wasn't always true, as you now know. Right now, I'm not really interested in taking on new clients. I'm focused on the slow money part of my own business for the current phase.

I can be even worse now. I tell people that I'm a celebrity ghostwriter and currently not taking new clients.

When things are scarce, people want them more and are willing to pay a premium. Sometimes, acting like a scarce resource, even when you're desperate for work, can land you the fee you need.

When you position yourself as an expert, you can expect to be paid higher rates, but you'll also start to be treated differently. People don't call specialists all the time; they save their calls for true emergencies. Do you think clients call me every day anymore? None of them even have my number.

## Take Action

Spend some time on UpWork and study what jobs have been hired out in your area of focus. Compare what people are paid on bidding platforms to what people get paid for one-on-one jobs.

Write down how you want potential clients and customers to perceive you. How can you create that reality quickly?

Will launching a book to the top of the charts increase

your perceived expertise? How about having a nice-looking website? Look for other experts in your chosen field who are getting paid the most. How do they position themselves and demand those high fees?

Put together an action plan to replicate their positioning.

# SELL IT THREE TIMES

I don't like to engage in any project unless I can get paid for my work three times. A perfect example of this is getting paid to take a training course, selling what I've learned as a service to clients, and then using that training to build my own website to generate my own revenue streams. That's three ways to get paid.

As you're looking at what assets you can leverage, whether it's a service, an asset, a skill, or a relationship, check first if you can profit from it three times. If you can sell a skill right now that won't help you grow your long-term online business, that's not good enough.

Look for skills and assets that will help you to grow your business. I can't recommend learning copywriting enough. If I could go back in time, this is the skill that I would learn first. If you go to my website, I have an entire training course on how you can become a master copywriter for free. It's a downloadable PDF. Enter your email address and I will send you a 600-page file that has hundreds of old highly successful advertisements from the 1880s through the early 1940s.

The beauty of copywriting is that you can learn it for free. You can have someone pay you to write your first sales letter. Then, when you get better at it, you can get paid more and write them for yourself to generate more revenue.

A large percentage of my revenue comes from my ability to write my own sales letters now. Like my personality, they're not perfect. I make a lot of mistakes in my videos, but they're real, earnest, and honest. I follow a formula that works.

We are going to delve deeper into skills and business models in the Ring of Void. That's where all these concepts will come together for you. Make sure that you are looking at the long term before you dive into the last element. Don't master a skill that will lose its value over time.

The perfect example of a dead-end skill is being good at MySpace. Fifteen years ago, that was awesome. Now, nobody knows what it is. Certain skills atrophy over time. If your skill is for a specific social media platform, that's a commodity.

Getting really good at Twitter is cool, but if Twitter goes out of business – any social media platform could turn into MySpace – suddenly, you have a skill that's no longer useful. But if your skill is communicating with people, designing videos, or writing scripts, those things are timeless.

Be strategic in the business model that you use to start generating fast money. As you do, I want you to always think of the rule of three:

Get paid before you do it.

Get paid while you do it.

Get paid after you do it.

## Take Action

Assess the skills from the Water Ring. Winnow out the skills that only have short-term value. You can leverage them now but don't invest time in improving them. Transition as quickly as possible to skills that can generate short and long-term revenue.

Mark the skills that will be valuable for you as you build up your slow money. Can you get paid three times? Will one client pay you to learn the skill, while the next pays you more for your expertise?

Refine the list of assets in your Breakthrough Journal using this new metric.

# 53

# RING OF FLAME REFLECTION
# QUESTIONS

1. In the past, has education been an investment with a financial burden attached to it?

2. How would you feel if you could graduate college with money in the bank instead of an albatross[1] of debt hanging around your neck?

3. Would having enough breathing room to build your business lower your stress levels?

4. How will you feel with diversified active income streams?

5. How does securing your own retirement make you feel?

6. Do you like the idea of depending on yourself instead of others as you age?

7. Have you sabotaged yourself in the past? Looking back, can you see why it happened now?

8. Does betting on yourself make you nervous or excited?

9. Are you ready to do whatever it takes to reach your goals? Even eat a little crow?

10. Were you hoping that the path to success would be paved in gold, or are you ready to fight through the mud to get the life you deserve?
11. Do you see me as an expert? Why is that?
12. How can you create the perception of expertise around you?
13. Which skill, asset, or resource can you leverage now for fast income?

# 54

# RING OF FLAME MASTERY

There is only one way to keep the fires of your passion burning, and that is to feed the flames. Nothing does the job quite like cold hard cash. Take the lessons from this section and take fast action. When I started my own journey, I posted an ad on Craigslist on Saturday and had a check in my fist by Thursday.

It's time to go beyond your Breakthrough Journal and take your fire out into the real world. Develop a plan to make your first dollar. Choose one of your assets using the metrics from this Ring and leverage it. Tell your friends, family, associates, and strangers about your offer. Post it to appropriate social media channels and websites.

Put in the work to get that first taste of fiery victory.

# ELEMENT FIVE VOID – BUSINESS MODELS

# 55

## SHAPELESS IN THE VOID

Welcome to the final Ring, Void. This is where we bring everything together with some powerful metaphors. After reading this section, you may find it worthwhile to re-read the previous sections as now they will make a lot more sense. The sections are called "rings" because they are circular and connect with each other. You can master the Rings in any order, so feel free to go back anytime you need to.

Void is the most powerful of the Rings because it is the least understood. Void is completely adaptable and can change shape to fit any situation. There is an old quote that may have become modified through translation from Japanese and through retellings across time. A martial arts master once commented that fighting with Jigoro Kano, the founder of Judo, was like fighting against an empty jacket.

This style of judo is called Aikido. With this martial art, you use all of your opponent's energy against them. They run at you, and you convert that energy into a flip. The less energy you expend, the more efficient you become. Using this technique, you can defeat hundreds of opponents without breaking a sweat. They are doing all the work for you.

In this Ring, we will discuss six powerful passive income business models. Each of them is very effective and a part of my primary business. I practice all six of these styles every single month to generate revenue.

Right now, you are formless and shapeless like the Void. As you learn about each business model, you will find the one that best fits your existing assets and your fast money strategy. That is where you will direct your energy until you master that business model.

When you combine a business model with your existing assets, you will develop the perfect plan. This is the section where everything will come together, and you can fully transition from learning to doing.

Void is the place in between. It is the place of nothingness. If you've seen or read *The Neverending Story*, you know how powerful nothing can be. It's not that nothing is a lack of something. The power is in its potential. In the void, you can create anything. You are limitless, and with your skills and imagination, anything is possible. When you master this Ring, you can create a business from your will alone. It's an exciting time, and I can't wait to see what you create!

# 56

# THE AUTHOR PATH

There are multiple business models that you can use to generate both fast and slow money. Our goal is to develop the same set of skills to do both of these tasks while being as lean and efficient as possible. The last thing you want to do is double your workload by learning and honing one skill for your fast money and a completely different one for your slow and long-term money.

The beauty of the author model is that there's a great deal of opportunity. Writing books and generating long-form content has always worked and will continue to work. It's exactly the business model that I follow for my primary business. I generate fast money by taking ghostwriting jobs and slow money by publishing my own books.

When you're deciding if this is the right business model for you, there is a very simple question you can ask yourself. Do you like writing? Do you like talking and generating long-form content?

It doesn't really matter how good you are at writing. There are loads of writers who are more eloquent and more talented than me, but because I'm methodical and consistent, I can generate massive amounts of good content and outperform them.

You'll become a better writer over time, and as your credibility goes up in one area, it increases your credibility in other areas. As my ghostwriting fee goes up, I have a larger budget to put into the creation of other projects and to pay for advertising for my self-published books. And as my self-published books gain more reputation, I can demand a larger fee as a writer.

When *Serve No Master* blasted the top of the charts, as you can imagine, my ghostwriting fee went up. Every time I hit a major success, whether it's financial or winning an award, it increases the amount of money I generate from each different part of my business.

As a writer, you will go through several business cycles. A great deal of your time is spent researching and writing books. Then you will spend time managing your book launches and working to generate as many sales as possible. With sales success, you will then grow a following and direct them to other courses on your website or more books in your series.

Even though I love writing, there is more to writing than just putting words on the page. The other business models all work in tandem with my writing to support my overall business.

## A Week in the Life of an Author

As an author, you start Monday morning assessing how your books performed over the weekend. In the mornings, you read emails from fans, check for newly discovered typos and correct them in your master files. You then check your social media channels to respond to all the messages that came in overnight.

Once you are caught up with your fans, it's time to check your outlines. You keep a notebook filled with books in different phases of creation. On one page you write down every new idea, and later in the notebook each idea gets a book title. Then you write one title on the top of each page and outline your books below.

Planning out your series and which books will come next is a big part of starting your week. If you are working with a publisher, you will update them on your current project, discuss if your book will be on time and review your book to make sure the final edition matches their expectations.

Whether you are getting feedback from an editor, publisher, or beta readers, you will spend time each week updating your current project.

Every week, you also spend time researching and planning the launches of your books, from selecting categories and keywords to reviewing cover designs.

To continue the growth of your books, you will track which ones are selling well and which ones are starting to dip. Tracking ad campaigns is an important weekly task. Are you making more than you are spending on ad campaigns? Is that campaign targeting your free book generating enough reads of your paid books to cover the costs?

Then it's time to generate engagement content. This can be emails, social media posts, blog posts, or podcasts that you deliver to keep your fans interested in your content in between book releases. You will check for other authors you want to cross-promote with. This can be a book swap, writing a foreword to their books, or simply posting on each other's social media channels or blogs.

After lunch, it's time to write. I find a nice slice of solitude to dictate for a few hours each day. You will find your own special spot where you can work on your next book and maintain your daily word count goals.

Once your new draft is finished, more of your weekly time will be spent on editing, rewriting, and changing parts of your book to get closer to the finished product.

You spend your week balancing time between talking to fans, marketing your books, and planning ways to grow your business.

## Case Study

Last week, I launched my first free book *Fire Your Boss*. I stretched my wings in a new direction as part of a marketing plan. I found some platforms where I can only exchange leads with authors if I have a book that is permanently free in digital form.

I started by examining the top free business books to see what they had in common and what people expect from a free book in terms of length, content, and quality.

From my research, I saw that I would either write a book about blogging or a list of business models. Those are the only two types of books that do well long-term in the free business category.

I studied the outlines of the top books I wanted to model and even read a few to get a feeling for what I wanted to create. Some books went really deep into detail on business models that I don't like, such as becoming a driver for Uber. Others had lists of hundreds of business models with links to a new course or product every few pages.

Both of these didn't appeal to me as extremes. For my book, I decided to cover 16 business models with a few pages on each. The total book length would be 20,000 words or less.

Once the book was outlined in my notebook, I began dictating. I dictated the entire book over a few days. The app that I use automatically syncs with Google Drive. However, the format is a weird one that no transcription program can read. After the dictation is complete, I go to my computer and convert the audio files into MP3s and give them names I can easily track in my records. I am very fastidious in my file names because I write so many books.

I then upload the audio files to my current favorite transcription software and share with my editor. She cleans up the files and edits them at the same time and delivers a completed Scrivener file for me to review.

While she is working on the first draft, I start working on the book cover with my design team. I found about ten stock images of beaches that I liked, sent the cover text to my designer and asked them to come up with some concepts.

They knocked it out of the park on the first try. This normally doesn't happen, but something just went right, and I loved the first concept.

I then started working on the front and back matter, deciding on the free gifts I would offer in exchange for an email address and how I would convert a reader of a free book into someone who buys either a book or a course from me.

I found an engaging chapter from *Serve No Master* and included that at the end of the book to entice them to transition into a paid book.

My book then came back from the editor, and I spent a few days on rewrites and tweaking my messaging. During rewrites, I find references for any quotes or facts that I put into the book. I want to back up any claims that I make, whether it is about how many people go to college and work minimum wage jobs or medical insurance stats for millennials.

Once the book is finalized in Scrivener and I'm happy with it, I send it back to my editor to polish and convert into Vellum format. That's the tool I use to format books that I self-publish. I then polish that file and add in the front and back matter. This is now the project's master file. Any typo corrections in the future will be to the Vellum file.

While I'm finalizing the book, I begin to plan how I will launch it. When the book is ready to publish, I have to prepare the description, keywords, and categories for all of my different channels. Once the book description is written, I convert it into HTML. I upload the book to each platform simultaneously and have to go through all of their approval processes before each edition is live.

Once the digital edition is live, I have to go through the manual process of converting it into a free book. I have to send them links to other places where the book is free and ask them to price-match. After a few days, they finally drop the price to free, and I can share the book with my following.

For this book, I decided to try delivering free copies using a Facebook Chatbot. Unfortunately, only 20 percent of people were able to see and click the button on that page, so that test didn't go very well.

It was a test with my loyal following, so it wasn't a total disaster, as I just sent them the link to free copies the next day.

Enough of my following were excited by my new free book that it shot up to the #1 free business book on the very first day. While this is exciting, the purpose of the book is to appeal to more than just my existing audience.

The real goal is to get enough of them to leave positive reviews that strangers will want to buy the book when they see it for free. With the book live and downloads slowing down from my current audience, I set up ad campaigns on two platforms to keep the book visible to as many people as possible.

My goal is to give away 200 copies of the book every day. I prefer long-term, consistent downloads to a single spike one day and crashing the next. I usually run two tests. One test is at $10 a day for five days, and the other test is at $5 a day with no end date. I will check the stats of each campaign weekly to see if I want to continue them and if there are increases in my email subscribers and sales to match the ad spend.

The next process will be to create giveaway pages where people can get the book for free from my website, participate in more free book swaps and giveaways and find other ways to get my free book into as many hands as possible.

While I'm managing that book's marketing, I'm also writing and finishing the final chapters for this book, *Breakthrough*. As an author, I never want to get tunnel vision and only work on one project at a time. I'm always trying to move the goal posts on multiple projects at the same time. That way I never have big delays between book releases.

## Take Action

Research how writing books could help the other parts of your business.

Then test yourself to see if you really like the idea of being an author. Write down ideas for twenty books in a series. This can be fiction or non-fiction. If you can see yourself writing twenty books on the same topic or following the same character, you might just have the heart of an author.

If the book series starts to seem like a lot of work by book five, then this might not be the perfect business model for you to start with. While many people who read this book will have the heart of an author, not all of you will.

# 57

# THE CONTENT CREATION PATH

O ur second business model is content creation. When I say content, I mean short-form content, no matter how you deliver it. It can be writing articles, creating memes for social media, recording videos, or doing voice-over work. There are loads of ways to generate content in the new economy.

You should choose whichever part of the spectrum matches your natural skill set. If you have a beautiful voice, lean into voice-over work like my friend Adam does.[1] If you are amazing using your phone or tablet to create social media content, such as graphics, videos, or even just little statements that can go viral, then lean into that.

It's impossible to do everything. Success as a content creator comes from leaning into your primary assets. Trying to master blog posts, videos, and voice-over work all at once will lead to disaster. There are many paths within content creation; find the one that best suits you.

People often ask why it's not my voice on my audio-books. The voice for *Serve No Master* is British, and he sounds amazing. I like having a different voice represent each of my books. I have no idea who is going to read this book, but if you're listening to the audiobook right now, I bet it sounds amazing.

Even though I dictate my books, I never am the voice on my audiobooks. It's a different skill that's far outside what I'm capable of doing. Even though I live on a tropical island, there's pretty much no such thing as absolute silence here, which is required when you're recording an audiobook. When you want to publish an audiobook on ACX, they run it through a computer program that checks the background noise, and I can tell you that during the initial recording of this chapter, I've heard roosters crow hundreds of times. I would not pass that check.

There is always someone planing a piece of wood, dogs fighting, or my kids screaming in the background. Those crazy background noises add character to my podcasts episodes but would never pass muster with Audible.

In addition to all the wild background noises, I don't have the patience to read back a book that I've already written and dictated. Voice-over work is hard, and I just don't have what it takes. I can't even read five-minute scripts without making mistakes or changing words on the fly, which isn't allowed with an audiobook. You have to read whatever is on the page, even if there is a mistake. You ignore it and keep going.

It's outside my skill set and interests, so I prefer finding other people with beautiful voices who can deliver something better than I could do on my own.

Voice-over work is just one of the many ways you can create content.

The beauty of content creation is that everything you do for clients you can then do for yourself. If you want to learn how to write blog posts or do voice-overs, take a job doing it for someone else and use that money to pay for the equipment and training you need.

While you might be at the bottom of the market when you get started, you can increase your income with each successive client. With basic equipment, you might only be able to charge $25 per finished hour, but as you raise money to soundproof your studio and get better microphones, you can work toward the top of the market where artists are paid more than $1,500 per finished hour.

You can get paid to learn this amazing craft with zero experience. I just sent an offer to a woman to read one of my books, and it didn't go through. Her profile wasn't completed on the audiobook platform, and an error popped up. She is so new that her profile isn't complete, and I still tried to give her the job.[2] I just sent her a message to complete her profile, so that I can hire her.

You might have noticed that I said "she." I used to only hire men to read my books under male author names and women for female author names. But I received a great audition last year from a woman who suggested I consider letting a woman read my book. I realized that people probably wouldn't mix up my gender when listening to the audiobook, as I mention my wife and having kids all the time, so I gave her a shot.

If the voice sounds good, funny, or inspiring, that person gets hired. This woman's audition reminded me of a character I liked on Scrubs[3] when I was in high school, so I had no choice but to send her an offer.

There is a lot of work as a short-form content creator. When I started out working online, one of my additional services was recording videos for clients that we would then post online to generate more links and traffic for their websites. I had very little experience with video cameras, but I did spend a year working on a BA in Sound Engineering.[4]

## A Week in the Life of a Content Creator

Your week begins with managing the content you've already put out there. This can mean responding to comments, checking email, and handling your social media channels. Whether you are creating content for yourself or a client, tracking progress is critical.

If you are working with clients, part of each week will be spent managing their expectations, asking them to provide you with text and graphical assets, and searching for new clients to maintain your revenue streams. Client management often involves phone calls to check in with clients and to confirm approval of your posts and content for the week.

For each content channel you are working on, you will have to map out your content at least a few weeks in advance, so that you have time to approve and release each piece on time. Scheduling apps that release your content on time will become your best friend.

Once you have your content needs for the week road mapped, you will spend time researching and prepping that content. For each piece of content, you will need banners, headers, and other graphics well in advance of the release date.

As part of the research process, you will decide which keywords need to be in your articles and which tags you should attach to your posts to connect to the hottest trends.

Once your prep work is complete, you can move into the content creation phase. Whether you are recording videos or writing blog posts, you will develop a replicable process. Each time I want to record a video, I prepare my gear in the same way, go to the same location, check that everything is working smoothly and then begin recording takes. I know that I will spend much of my time dealing with strange background noises on the beach, including dog fights, children shouting, and strangers talking to me as they walk by.

As you develop your rhythm, you will become familiar with your usual hurdles and find ways to overcome them. I prepare my content as far in advance as I can, so that I'm never under time pressure to record. As you get more organized, you can spend this week working on videos and articles for next month.

## Case Study

My biggest area of content creation is videos for my Facebook group. I put out a new video every single day to my group. The process begins with a month's worth of ideas from my group manager. She comes up with ideas and questions that other members of the group have been asking or she thinks will be valuable.

Each day of the week, I post a video on a specific topic, so the videos are organized by topic rather than linearly.

I record all the book writing videos, then all the podcasting videos, and then the networking videos, etc. I usually record a month of videos in a single two-hour marathon session.

Once the videos are recorded, I send them to my group manager via Dropbox. She will set the publishing date in advance and deliver the content daily to my audience.

Once the videos are uploaded, they spark discussion, and I check on the threads every day.

Sometimes, your content creation will focus on a larger

project. I was recently invited to write a guest post for a website with a much larger following than mine.

The process began with me building a relationship with the website owner over the past few years. I'm an affiliate for one of his software tools that I use daily, so it's easy for me to recommend it.

As we were chatting on Skype a few months ago, I asked about how he generates guest content. He said he'd love to have an article written by me and gave me a list of choices. From that list, I selected a topic I was interested in. It was about avoiding copyright violations with your book covers.

I'm fascinated by this topic, and I don't want any of my followers to get in trouble when they misuse an image, so I started researching.

The first draft of the article took me three days to write. I sent it to my father, who is a retired lawyer, to get his opinion. Because copyright law is changing all the time, there were certain cases where the final answer was murky.

We sent the article back and forth three times and spoke on the phone for several hours so that we both knew exactly what we wanted the article to convey and to give the best information possible without actually giving legal advice.

After a few weeks of working on the article together, I sent it to my editor. Once she was done with her changes, I sent it to the website owner where the article will be posted.

He then sent it to his article manager, and they went through their review and edit processes. Six weeks later, they emailed me to say the article would be published the next week and mailed to their following of 60,000 people.

Because the article was so in-depth, they are allowing me to link to a landing page rather than my website homepage. Everyone who reads my article and wants to learn more will be sent to a page where they can get a free copy of *Fire Your Boss* after they enter their email address.

As a content creator, your time is balanced between finding clients, planning future content, creating that content, and managing its release.

## Take Action

When you looked at the author business model, was it the idea of writing a full book or simply the act of writing that you didn't like about it?

I'm terrible at ghostwriting articles. Writing short-form doesn't match my natural skill set, but it might match yours.

Creating videos, recording audio, drawing comics, and creating memes are all really valuable right now. If these are in your wheelhouse, I would love for you to email me. That's how most people end up interning or working for me.

There are loads of amazing business people who are weak where you are strong, and you will be pleasantly surprised at the opportunities that crop up when you lean into your strongest asset.

Take a look at this business model and write down the style of content creation that appeals to you. If you like this business model, create a business plan.

What kind of Flame Ring tasks will you do to generate fast money? What will you charge? How will you generate your first clients? Did you realize that blogging falls into this category?

How will you transition from client work to long-term passive income streams?

Even writing out a single-paragraph business model will help you to solidify this plan.

# 58

# THE ARBITRAGE PATH

The third business model is arbitrage, the buying and reselling of assets, resources, or skills. Most successful and wealthy online marketers have discovered that the middle is the best place to be.

There are many ways you can buy and resell online at a premium. An example of the online arbitrage business model is to buy traffic from Facebook in the form of advertising and then resell it to someone else in the form of promoting their offer for a commission. If you can spend a dollar for a block of traffic and sell that same block for a dollar and one penny, you already have a simple and scalable business model.

Another thing you can buy and sell online is services. When I first started online marketing, I sold SEO[1] services. I didn't know anything about it, but I learned how to rank websites to the top of the search results. I got paid to learn how to do it and used that money for training, courses, and software. Once I got results from my clients' websites, I was also able to rank up my own websites and use them to get more clients at a higher price point.

The process of ranking a website is a commodity. It's a series of tasks that anyone can do. I was spending ten to fourteen hours a day doing these tasks. Eventually, I realized that if I paid someone else to do the work, I could spend more time on client acquisition. When I did all of the SEO work myself, I couldn't handle more than ten clients at a time. This capped my earning potential, and I had a non-scalable business model. It might pay the bills, but I would never be wealthy.

After this revelation, I moved from pure service delivery into arbitrage. I stopped doing the work myself and worked with a company that provided white label service, which means that they do the work and I put my logo on it. This works for nearly every online service, and that's what most people do.

Arbitrage can be used for products as well as services. There is no Amazon where I live, but you can shop online at a local version of it. Most of the sellers on there are simply practicing arbitrage. They find an item on AliExpress and relist it on the local site for a higher price. They add in a premium for being the middleman. They copy the images and description from one website and paste them into another before raising the price.

They never even open the package. Half the time, my deliveries are still in Chinese packaging with the original Chinese shipping labels. Arbitrage isn't a secret. People will often pay a premium for convenience.

These sellers don't order anything until they receive an order, which means they don't have any capital expenditures. If no one buys anything, they don't spend anything, so the risk is low. That's the beauty of arbitrage.

I still do arbitrage all the time. People approach me for help editing their books, planning a product launch, or writing a sales letter. They'll often pay a certain fee because of my name and reputation when, in fact, someone on my team does 90 percent of the work, and I just check it. As long as I'm the one answering the phone, the client doesn't care who performs the work.

You can grow to a point where people want your agency but what they are really paying for is the security of your brand and your level of knowledge.

You can sell services and get other people to do the work behind the final product. Sometimes, you just have to do the project management or organization.

As one warning from my experience, you should always charge at least triple because clients often run over budget and change what they want.[2]

For example, you might know nothing about technical web design, but if someone were to ask you to design a website for them, you could post the job on a design forum like UpWork. Choose the proposal that impresses you the most, change it to your name, and show it to the potential client. If they like that work, you tell them it will cost triple whatever that designer bid. If the client doesn't like the initial proposal, you can always tell them you lead multiple web design teams and show them another designer's proposal.

Even if you told the potential client you were hiring a team on UpWork, they probably wouldn't care. There are a lot of people that will gladly pay a higher price to have a local manager handling the task even though they could pay less to outsource directly.

The ability to find a team in India or Eastern Europe is a valuable skill, and that comes with experience. Simply by being a local agent or representative, you can sell loads of different services, ranging from graphic design to SEO services. You can often hire someone to do the task using Fiverr, UpWork, or other gig economy platforms. Arbitrage really is that simple.

The real value for any company is working as a rain-maker.[3] If you spend all of your time delivering the services yourself, you don't have enough time for more clients, and you max out.

Arbitrage is the way you will scale many of these business models. I can only write a certain number of books per month myself, but I can subcontract significantly more ghostwriters. The important part of arbitrage is to check the work of anyone you hire to work under your name.

With arbitrage, having someone else do the actual service work, ten clients or one hundred would take the same amount of my time. Arbitrage unlocks scalability.

### A Week in the Life of an Arbitrager

You start each week by going over the previous week's stats. Are you onboarding new clients? Have any complaints come in? Did all of your clients' payments clear?

You don't want to pay a vendor for a client who stopped paying you.

A great deal of your time every week is spent managing clients and ensuring that they are happy with the service you are delivering. Additionally, you have to track all of your revenue streams. For some projects, you won't get paid for months, so you must put notes into your calendar to check that the payments arrive when they are due.

If you are delivering a service, such as SEO, many clients will want to spend some time on the phone with you each week.

Once you have handled all your current projects, it's

time to start prospecting. This can mean designing advertisements, posting signs in your community, or running ads on Facebook. You should have a firm understanding of your lifetime client value and keep a steady flow of new clients into your funnel to maintain your revenue numbers.

Once you have your traffic sources updated, it's time to start closing clients. This means a lot of time on the phone, emailing, using chat tools and even meeting in person.

In meetings with potential clients, you will have to take them through your sales process, manage expectations, use your closing tools, and set up payment in an efficient manner. This can mean pulling out a credit card swiper that you attach to your phone or setting up a recurring payment online.

Once you have that first payment, you need to take clients through an onboarding process that lasts at least a week. This is so that if they are late with a payment in the future, you don't accidentally pay the vendor to keep servicing them. The client will receive delayed services, and it's critical that you manage their expectations during this time. You need that buffer in place.

As you continue to close clients, more of your time will be taken up managing those existing clients and checking to ensure that your vendors are delivering high-quality services. If your white label team starts slacking, you can lose all of your clients in one fell swoop.

Most of your time in arbitrage is spent talking to people, either setting up deals, finding clients, or managing vendors.

## Case Study

One of the biggest issues with new authors is that they design terrible covers. It kills their book sales. I have put out multiple free and paid trainings on the issue, and it doesn't seem to matter.

Even when clients pay me thousands of dollars, they will slap a garbage cover on a book and ignore my advice. Then they are shocked when nobody buys the book.

I use a great service for my graphics, and with every deliverable, they include an editable version.

I combined my need for better covers for my audience with my access to cheap and editable graphics files. There hasn't been a good set of book cover templates released in a few years, so I know there is also a gap in the market.

I created a folder on my computer and began saving great book covers from each category. Once I had one hundred covers that I wanted to model, I found stock photos I wanted to use with each template, and then I created a set of instructions for my designers.

I wanted each cover to be easy to edit, come with the necessary fonts, and fit every category out there.

My next complaint about most book templates is that they don't include an audiobook template. While book covers are rectangles, audiobooks are squares, like CD cases. For each of my templates, my designers are creating an eBook cover, a print cover, and an audiobook cover.

I then built a membership area and recorded a short sales video. With only twenty of the eBook covers completed, I ran a test sale to my audience and generated almost $500 in sales in one day. This confirmed that the idea was a good one, and my designers are continuing to make more covers every single day.

While this is a small initial sales number, it covers most of my costs in getting the covers designed. Every sale after the official launch will be pure profit – and, of course, they provide a needed and useful resource for many new authors out there with covers that aren't selling. This form of arbitrage is buying a product from someone else and selling it on your own while reaping all the profits.

## Take Action

Does the thought of buying and selling appeal to you or does it feel a little sleazy? Most sellers on online marketplaces, auction houses, and drop-shippers are just practicing arbitrage. When you go to the mall and buy something from a store, that store is practicing arbitrage. They buy the item from the manufacturer and sell it to you. That's why wholesale pricing is so much lower than retail.

This business model has existed for a very long time.

What gets you more excited, finding clients or doing the actual work? Do you like closing deals or burning the midnight oil to finish a project?

If your strongest asset is your friends and social network, you might be a natural fit for arbitrage.

# 59

# THE MADE TO ORDER PATH

I find this model fascinating because you can sell physical things that don't exist until your customers order them.

Warehouses can be stressful. The thought of having a big stack of anything sitting on a shelf somewhere, and I have to sell it or I get in trouble would make me nervous. I have loads of products that I've only sold one or two of, and because I designed them as print-on-demand, there's no loss.

Some of my ideas have failed. I've designed courses and written books that just didn't work. When an idea doesn't work out, the main loss is opportunity cost and time. There are ways to minimize that by testing an offer before creating it, but if I wanted to print a hundred books, I would have to sell them all, or I've lost money on the project. That's a huge amount of pressure.

My wife and I just ordered fifty custom surfing shirts for our hostel.[1] We had to pay all the money upfront, and we won't get our money back until we sell twenty-five of them. The second half might be all profit, but the first half is all stress. This is the first time I've ever had to order stock, and it feels very unnatural to me.[2]

The beauty of printing on demand is that it applies to almost every type of product and service you can think of. If it's not something you can print in a one-off, there's often an opportunity to sell using someone else's warehouse. You buy at a wholesale price and sell it at retail price.[3]

There are some amazing things you can do with 3D printers. There are machines now that print metal. You can create almost anything with modern machines. There are now CNC machines that carve metal into any shape you want. Throw in a block of metal, tell it to make a hammer, and it'll make a perfect hammer – better than anything you could buy at the hardware store. It's amazing. The sky is the limit when it comes to clothes. You can print on demand just about anything you want.

I worked on a project with one of the greatest inventors in the world,[4] and he's a big believer in how easily you can test and prototype products now using 3D printing. You can test your ideas for a few hundred dollars before you launch it, rather than the tens of thousands it would cost to create prototypes just a decade ago.

Made to order has democratized the physical universe. You can create and sell products without having to build them first. You no longer need a massive bank loan to cover your first production run.

You can build a huge catalog of designs and items without needing any warehouse space. You can run everything out of your bedroom. Print on demand is only going to get better, and your creativity is truly the limit.

## A Week in the Life of Making to Order

You start every week checking your statistics. How many orders went through and how many came in? Is everything running smoothly with your deliveries? Is your backend delivering products on time? Have there been any returns or complaints from customers?

Once you catch up on the weekend, it's time to check your process from start to finish. Is your traffic staying consistent or growing? Do you need to increase your advertisement budget?

Once you've checked your traffic flows, you will analyze your product suite. Which products are selling and which are failing? You want to focus on the winners and possibly shut down the losers.

Once you're happy that the right products are getting the attention they need, it's time to track your vendors. Are they charging you correctly or can you find a better place to have your products made for less? Is their team handling customer support or yours?

You will sell your products through several modes – directly through social media, on your own website, and on larger platforms like Amazon, Ebay, and Etsy. As you gather customers from other platforms, your goal is to keep moving them to your website so that you don't have to share the profits from each sale.

You will work to build a contact database, write emails, and set up sales and promotions to get people excited to buy directly from you rather than the larger store where they found you.

After you have worked on the logistics of your business, it's time to focus on the creative side. You will need to develop a steady stream of ideas from text to graphics. Then you have your artist or design team come up with mockups. You will spend a lot of time sending them your ideas, studying their concept art, asking for changes, approving art, and finally adding it to your product offerings.

This business has a lot of moving parts, and your job is to make sure they are all connected together as your business grows.

If you're working for clients, you will spend time each week finding new clients, managing them, and getting approval for artwork. Whether you are working with bands, local businesses, or small sports teams, they will each have their own budgets, logos, and approval processes. You might be speaking to the manager of a baseball team one week and a high school principal the next.

Selecting the best place to build each of your products is a big part of your process, and you will spend time emailing factories in America and in China. Comparing international shipping costs to labor costs will help you choose where to get your products made.

When you have a winner, you will test ways to scale it. Should you run more ads, put the same design on different items, or come up with new ideas for the same customers? Will a shirt design look as good on a hat? Will people buy it in a different color?

Because your products are shipped straight from the vendor to your customers, you can't personally manage quality control. That means keeping an eye on every email, comment, and review from your customers so that you can catch a glitch before it grows into a nightmare.

**Case Study**

Earlier this year, I had an idea for a shirt, but I didn't know if anyone else would like the concept. My business is called Serve No Master, and there is a Japanese word synonymous with this concept: ronin. A ronin is a masterless samurai, and while being masterless was considered low in feudal Japan, it's what we all aspire to nowadays.

In the past, I have tested other ronin concepts, and they didn't do well. Many of my followers don't know this word, even though it was the name of a big film in the 1990s. I lived in Japan for a long time, and my Japanese is passable, so my familiarity with Japanese terms is not the norm.

Rather than printing hundreds of shirts to see if anyone wanted them, I decided to run a test to my following. I sent a few samurai stock images to my designers with the text "Modern ronin, I work for myself." The design they sent back was awesome.[5]

I was really excited, but there was a challenge. Most of my followers are older than me. While I was a child of the eighties and grew up on *The Karate Kid* and *Mortal Kombat*, many of my followers are from a generation before that and have less fascination with the Far East.

The final question became, "Would my followers buy a shirt with an intense feudal design on the front?"

Ninety percent of the shirts I wear are blank. I've become boring, and what I like isn't always the same as what my followers like.

I decided to run a promotion for one week where I would sell as many shirts as possible and see how my followers responded. If the shirt was a champion, I could then run paid advertising campaigns.

I used a T-shirt company that lets you run timed offers

and handles everything from payment processing to fulfillment and customer service. They do *everything* once you upload your design. All I did was send emails and wait for a direct deposit after the campaign was done.

While we only had a few sales, the cost-to-profit ratio was very strong for this test. The design cost me $7.50 and about fifteen minutes of my time, and the campaign generated a profit of $30.90.

While this isn't the largest number, there were multiple hurdles. Some people wanted different colors, others wanted the design on the back, and other people wanted a different design altogether. This is where depth of product offering comes in to play. I have many more designs available now on my ecommerce store. I am constantly adding new designs and share the link with my audience whenever I want to boost sales.

While this is a small part of my business, it's very cool to see an idea go from design to something people wear. And it looks awesome!

## Take Action

There are many ways you can dive into print on demand, from books to putting faces on mugs to jewelry. Take some time and research the possibilities. Is there a specific sector of print on demand that gets you excited? Was there an idea you had in the past that has become feasible with new technology?

Write down the results of your research and your rough business plan in your Breakthrough Journal.

# 60

# THE RAINMAKER PATH

The middleman (or middlewoman or middleperson) is the epitome of the Void Ring. You never actually do anything. You use other people's energy to create wealth.

As a middleman, you get paid simply for your relationships. In my industry, there's a standard fee of 10 to 20 percent for an introduction. If you introduce two people to each other – one with a massive following and one with an amazing product – and they generate a million dollars in sales, you'll be paid between $100,000 and $200,000. And this is not considered grotesque; it's standard.

There are lots of different names for this job. Whether you call yourself an introducer, connector, JV broker, or launch manager, this is a person who doesn't create anything. But their ability to find great things to sell and combine them with people who want to buy those things is infinitely valuable.

I will gladly pay 10 percent introduction fees all day long. In fact, I have it built automatically into my software.

I'm a big fan of this type of marketing, which is sometimes called "tier two" marketing.[1]

Let's say I have a product that costs $100. If you talk your friend into buying it, you and I will split the money. We each earn $50. However, if your friend then tells someone else about that same product, you get a 10 percent introduction fee. You get ten bucks, your friend gets fifty, and I get forty. And we all walk away happy.

While you make less money per sale, you will generate a much larger volume of sales that makes up for the difference.[2]

I love introducing people and generating tiny trickles of revenue that sometimes turn into tsunamis of profit. The most expensive course I sell on my website is my networking course. Unfortunately, it's the training that the fewest people buy because it's hard to perceive its value.

I can say, "Build a blog," "Sell a product at this price point," "Get this much traffic," or "This is how much money you'll generate from blogging," and it's clear what will happen when you complete the course.

Networking is an invisible skill, so it's hard for many people to assess its real value, but it's where you can make huge money. You can just go to conferences, meet everyone, build up a Rolodex, and all you do is introduce people to each other whenever they need someone with a matching skill set and take your percentage.

This business model doesn't require you to be technologically savvy. It doesn't even require you to sit in front of a computer all day long. You can spend all day in coffee shops, on the phone, going to the movies with people, and even playing golf because it's the depth of that relationship that leads to the connection.

This works on me, too. There are people who reach out to me and because of the level of relationship I will promote something they bring to me, even if I'm hesitant about it being the right fit. The stronger the relationship, the less I need to look at the numbers. There's real value in developing your network.

## A Week in the Life of a Rainmaker

The majority of your time is spent communicating with people. Rather than dealing with clients, you are focused on people with audiences and products to sell. Your greatest asset is your list of contents, and keeping those relationships fresh is critical.

You start each week by checking your emails, social media messages, tweets, texts, and every other way people like to communicate. I have many chat apps that I only use to communicate with a single person.

Once you've caught up on all the messages that have come in over the weekend, it's time to start planning out your weeks. If you are working for a client and managing a product launch or recruiting affiliates, you have to check in on them.

First, you will work to recruit as many people as possible to promote the offer. That means sending out emails and calling people to confirm they are on board.

That confirmation is the beginning of your job, not the end. Once people are on board, you have to call, email, and chase them down to keep them from forgetting when your promotion window opens. You have to provide them with social media images, descriptions of the products, and swipe emails they can copy and send to their followings.

When a promotion is live, you have to track who sends emails, if they send to their entire following or just a segment, and if the numbers are performing. If someone fails to mail, you have to pick up the phone and see what's going on.

When you're not in an active launch, you will be working to improve and increase your relationships. This means going to conferences and events. Shaking hands, remembering people's kids' names, and buying rounds of drinks are all a critical part of your business.

Because this is social calling, you will spend more time on your phone and at events than you will in your office. You can run your entire business from a phone, and deal making is your middle name.

You won't work regular hours because you have to adapt to the times your clients can meet you.

Your job boils down to how well you can meet new people, build rapport, and, most importantly, get them to like you. This career allows you to make money without building products or being technical. Your soft skills are far more valuable. And for all those efforts, you take home 10 to 20 percent of every deal you touch.

When you think of this career, think of the lawyer who never puts on a suit. My friend Jordan has an amazing story. A friend from law school brought him to his first law firm, but Jordan never saw him in the office. He finally discovered that his friend made more money finding clients for the law firm than he ever would writing briefs or arguing cases.

**Case Study**

I only travel to the United States once a year for a conference held in San Diego in the dead of winter. Most years, I throw a party at this conference for the sole purpose of staying on people's minds, building up goodwill, and, of course, having an amazing time.

At my party two years ago, I introduced my friend Charles to my buddy Steve. Charles has an amazing webinar on time management. He teaches people how to effectively use Evernote to save hours of time every single week.

At the end of his training webinar, he sells a course teaching his system. Steve decided to share this program with his audience. They loved the training.

Just for introducing two guys at my party, I was able to set up a deal that earned me a nice commission for $433.60. I didn't send one email, make one phone call or speak to a single client. Just introducing two people who worked together on a small project put money directly into my bank account.

## Take Action

Go back to that asset list you built in the Ring of Water. Are you impressed with your relationship assets, or is that where you are weakest? Can you see yourself leveraging those relationships into real revenue?

Write down your fast money business idea. Can you introduce two people now that will generate money for all three of you? Stop reading this and go introduce them right now!

# 61

# THE AFFILIATE PATH

The sixth but by no means final business model is the affiliate journey. With this model, it's harder to generate fast money, but the long-term passive income is amazing. With arbitrage, you get paid right away, before you even find the vendor. With print on demand, you get paid before you even plug in the 3D printer. As a middleman, you can charge an upfront fee before you even introduce two people.

But with affiliate marketing, you won't get paid until you generate the sale. There are CPA (cost per action) networks that will pay you when a customer inputs their zip code, home address, phone number, or email address. They pay more money for more information, but the payment per individual is very small. You need massive amounts of traffic and money to get into the CPA game.

I prefer getting paid a larger commission for every sale I generate. Every time someone buys a piece of software that I use or review of on my website, I get paid a percentage. It's easy to start chasing dollar signs and promote whatever

pays you the most – that's a real temptation with this business model, but you'll start to notice the value of integrity.

I don't have the biggest following in the world, but every
single person who has read one of my books, received one of
my emails, or visited my website knows that I don't recommend or review products that I don't actually use. When I
stop using a product, I stop recommending it. If a service I
used to like changes, and the quality drops, I will start
recommending someone better, even if they don't pay me
the biggest commission.

Integrity means people will trust you and go shopping
through a link you provide because they believe in you. You
get more sales because of your integrity. You can offer
services in the affiliate marketing world that are usually
generated through the other five business models we talked
about.

You can write review posts for someone else's blog to learn
and master the structure of a well-written review. There's a craft
and a science to writing reviews that not only demonstrates
expertise and gives people valuable information but also
encourages them to click the button at the end of the article.[1]

Affiliate marketing can be a powerful tool in your arse-
nal. As you get better at it, things get easier. There is a way to
generate some fast money, and that's to start being efficient
with what you recommend. Every time you recommend a
movie to your friends on a social media platform, if you use
a tracking link, you can get paid when someone watches or
buys the movie you liked.[2]

There are services and tools that I recommend on my
website that don't have an affiliate program. If it's the best,
it's the best, and I'm still going to recommend it. That's what
makes it easy to maintain your sense of self and not feel like

you're selling out because you only recommend products you've used and you know are good. This business model turns you into an authority that people trust.

A fascinating market is the world of video game reviews. There was a shake-up a few years ago when it turned out that most of the websites that review video games generate their revenue by selling ads and using affiliate links from those same video games. That's why most video games are rated about 20 percent higher by professional reviewers than they are by the people who actually buy and play that video game.[3]

This 20 percent dishonesty gap can be explained by their revenue stream. If you have a job writing for one of these big video game websites, and you write a bad review of a game that's one of their primary sponsors, that review might get spiked, and you'll probably get fired.[4]

This means that there's room for independent video game reviewers to leave honest reviews. Because they're not beholden to one of these larger brands, they can still generate revenue through their affiliate sales by being honest. Consumers will follow you because they want the honest lowdown. The real value comes from saying what you don't like. If you recommend everything, then no one trusts you.[5]

No matter your age, there are people looking for honest reviews, and they prefer a review by a person to one by an institution. That's why movie posters use the name of the reviewers as well as the website. You can build a brand teaching people of your generation about the products you are passionate about.

As an affiliate, your reputation is everything, and you make money based on the power of your recommendation.

As your reputation and following increase, your revenue will follow suit.

## A Week in the Life of an Affiliate

As an affiliate, your job is to always stay on the cutting edge of hot and popular trends. Your week will start with checking all your existing campaigns. You will look to see if your traffic is working well, if your ad campaigns are consistent, and if your vendors paid out on time. Depending on the products and services you promote, you might have to wait 90 days to get paid.

Some vendors might think you'll forget to check your numbers, and you have to keep your eyes peeled for that. If anyone is late paying, it's time to send a strongly worded email and pick up the phone. Expect to hear problems about frozen PayPal accounts, sick family members, and issues with the tracking software.

Once you've forced the people who owe you money to pay on time, it's time to see if you are promoting the best offers. You will start by looking at new offers trending on popular affiliate platforms. Then you will look at what your competitors are promoting and which paid advertising campaigns are currently being scaled on Facebook.

Once you have a new batch of campaigns that you're interested in, it's time to choose where to focus your energy. Your week might be spent writing emails, recording video reviews, or building custom bonuses to promote a new product.

If there is a new launch, you can reach out to the owner or their affiliate manager for an early copy so that you can have a review ready to go on day one. Building a custom bonus is critical, as many savvy online shoppers will search for the best bonus or discount they can find when making the decision to buy.

Then it's time to write or record your reviews, build your bonuses, and write your blog posts and emails.

Promoting great products is not a passive business. When you find an offer that your following responds to, it's time to contact the owner. Get them on the phone or at least a chat program and ask them to increase your commission. Most of the time, simply for asking, they will raise your payout by 10 percent.

You don't even have to give them a reason; they will figure it's worth it to keep your customers coming in.

In addition to all of the big picture work, there is plenty of time spent on the computer. You will create custom tracking links for each offer you promote. You want to know if a customer purchased because of a video on YouTube, a blog post on your website, or an email you sent out.

Knowing where your sales are coming from will help you to focus your future campaigns on the right traffic sources and to scale your business.

You will also spend time each week growing your traffic, from growing your YouTube following to improving your SEO to tweaking paid advertising campaigns.

The affiliate journey is a great place to start your online career.

## Case Study

Successful affiliate deals can be large or small. When I was first starting out, I had a following but no products to sell them. At a conference, I was implementing the principles of the master networker/middleman, and I met a guy named Jason.

He had a ton of products and was looking for more customers. I explained that I love promoting other products, but I didn't want to damage my relationship with my followers at the time by promoting products I didn't know anything about.

The first thing that I learned is that affiliates get tons of free stuff. He gave me free copies of his software and training programs worth thousands of dollars. He also set me up with lifetime commissions – any customer I sent to him would be tracked as mine for as long as they bought things.

After becoming a better marketer and using the resources from Jason, I started sending him customers. He had a free gift on a landing page, and I promoted it all day long. It was a great book and very valuable.

For the next year, I promoted Jason's products while I learned to build my own, and in that time, he paid me over $100,000. It was a massive amount of money and showed me the power of finding the right products to promote as an affiliate. It's the reason I offer lifetime commissions to anyone who promotes my products now.

Jason eventually changed his business structure, and I stopped promoting his products, but even though I haven't sent him a single new lead in five years, I get a residual check every couple of months for a few hundred dollars.

I know that not every affiliate promotion is going to be a unicorn; some are small but still lovely. A few years ago, I was promoting a small website host that I had a few sites with. Their service deteriorated, and my followers were starting to complain.

The moment the first email complaint came my way, I stopped promoting that service. I also became suspicious because their records claimed I had never sent them a customer.

While it's possible that a customer might have bypassed my tracking link, what happened next leads me to believe something else was going on.

After this bad experience, I found a new low-priced web host with a good set of reviews. I signed up for an account with them and set up a small website to test the customer experience. Everything was impressive, and the onboarding process was quite smooth.

I replaced my old affiliate links with new ones. Just changing a few screenshots in my blog post on how to set up your blog and replacing the links from one service with another led to a few sales each month.

I don't actively promote this service with emails or social media images. They are just a link on my resources page, and I mention them in my blog training courses. I decided to take my own advice and sent an email to their team asking for an increase in my commission. They checked over my blog post and tools page and decided I was going a good enough job. They bumped me from $65 a referral to $75. That's a 13 percent increase just for sending one little email.

In the past year, they have paid me $1,165 just for having their link in my resources section.

**Take Action**

Research your areas of expertise and passion. Are there tools you use that have killer affiliate programs? Can you get paid well to recommend the things that you already like to talk about?

Do you like writing in-depth reviews and explaining

exactly why you liked a movie, tool, piece of software, or game?

In your Breakthrough Journal, create a list of ten products or services that you would recommend at the start of your affiliate journey. How much would you make for each sale you generate? Are those numbers enough to pay the bills, or is the affiliate journey better used as a secondary revenue stream?

# 62

## ONE RING TO RULE THEM ALL

These are the six primary business models that I recommend to use to breakthrough with your business. As you went through your assessments, you may have discovered that you have a very specific skill that doesn't quite fit into one of these. You might be an outlier,[1] but most people who read this book will find that one of these paths is the perfect fit.

The beauty of these paths is that they don't require a lot of money upfront. The most expensive business model of all of these costs less than $100 to initiate. The era of borrowing twenty-five grand from the bank for a small business loan and spending the rest of your life sweating under that crippling debt is gone.

There are simple business models you can work on, no matter how much runway you have. If you only have two hours a week, just lost your job, or are living on a fixed income, it may change which of these paths you go down, depending on how quickly you need to generate revenue. But overall, these are the business models that I practice. That's why it's what I teach.

Each of these models can work in tandem with the others. Like a ring, they all strengthen each other. You can start with working as an author and use content creation to grow your following. You can use your work as a middleman to fund your print-on-demand projects. That's the beauty of the Breakthrough system; no matter which path you start with, it will strengthen the others.

# 63

# RING OF VOID REFLECTION QUESTIONS

1. Do you like writing?
2. Does the thought of people calling you a bestselling author put a smile on your face?
3. Would having your name on a bestselling book increase your credibility?
4. How do you feel about writing someone else's story?
5. Does the thought of creating a short piece of content appeal to you more than writing a long book?
6. Can you see yourself leveraging small pieces of content into fast revenue?
7. Do you get excited by the thought of hunting for clients and closing deals?
8. Are you more extroverted or introverted?
9. Are you looking for a path that will allow you to do most of your work in isolation?
10. How does the thought of selling something a customer can hold in their hands make you feel?

11. Does the idea of someone wearing a shirt you designed get you excited?

12. Does the thought of spending all your time connecting with people and developing relationships get you excited, or does it feel like a chore?

13. Can you see yourself networking all the time or part of the time to accelerate your business, or does it sound like a nightmare?

14. Does getting paid to recommend the things you love sound like a lot of fun?

15. Do you like researching amazing deals and sharing that information?

16. Can you see how these six models all work together to form an amazing business?

# 64

# RING OF VOID MASTERY

It's time to bring together everything you've learned in this Ring. If you participated in all of the smaller activities along the way, then this one will be easier for you. If not, this is your chance to catch up.

Investigate the different models and choose the one that best matches your previous research. Find a business model that gets you excited, can leverage your existing assets, can generate fast money, and you see yourself doing for a long time.

Once you have chosen the business model you will start with, it's time to turn that model into a business plan. Create a new page in your Breakthrough Journal called "Master Plan." On this page, please list:

- All existing assets
- How much runway you have
- Your first financial target
- How you will generate fast cash
- What you will charge

- How you will leverage that fast cash into more runway
- How you will generate passive income
- How you will get paid to learn
- How you will get paid three times
- Secondary skills and assets that will support this business
- The second business model you will use to accelerate your primary revenue stream

Once you have completed your master plan, it's time to implement it!

# CONCLUSION

You've made it this far in the journey, and that's very exciting for me. I appreciate the amount of time you've invested with me. Every single word you read was carefully organized to provide you maximum value in the minimum amount of time. Your time is valuable, and the fact that you've spent it with me reading this book means a lot to me. I don't want to let you down. I'm invested in your success.

Many times, I have bet it all on myself and gone all in, such as when I lost my job, launched my first online product when all my credit cards and bank accounts were frozen, and bought a hotel with my wife in a country where I didn't have permanent residency yet.[1] I know what it's like to feel a lot of pressure – to wonder if you're going to make ends meet, when you have people relying on you.

I want you to know that you're not alone anymore. You can connect with me through the Facebook group, my email list, and my website. You can start the way most people do and say, "Jonathan, I emailed you because I wanted to see if you really reply personally." I get that email five to ten times a week and it's my favorite because it's always followed by an amazing message.

I love communicating with my readers, and I want you to see that this is not a monologue. It's a dialogue. This is not me shouting and then disappearing. It is the beginning of a conversation. This is an action book. It isn't designed to make you feel good. My intention is to make you feel whatever emotion spurs you into action. If that's hope, great. If that's angst, I'll take that too.

If a year from now you've generated real online revenue, and you've broken through your barriers, it doesn't matter what emotion you felt at the end of this book. I'm building a tribe, not a friendship. That means I'm surrounding myself with people that are on the same journey, and success is the only measure. Nothing else matters.

The only measurement of the success of this book is if it works in the implementation, and that means it's time for you to take action. I hope you have taken action throughout this book – going through the activities and writing things down in your Breakthrough Journal. You should have completed all the assessments by now and have a deep understanding of how much money you need to generate, how much runway you have, and which skills, assets and talents you can leverage to change your life. If you haven't done those things, please go back and do them before you put down this book.

The only way you know you're doing something right is if you have some naysayers. If a book has 100 percent five-star reviews, something suspicious is going on. If this book turns out like my previous books, there will be people at the two ends of the spectrum. There will be people who read the book, take action and leave five-star reviews. And then there are people who don't try the activities, make excuses for their inaction and then have the audacity to leave a one-star review.

You have the right to do that, but it's intellectually dishonest. You don't whether *Breakthrough* works because you didn't try. If you buy a piece of furniture from IKEA and never try to assemble it, you can't leave a bad review and say it's the worst table you've ever seen. You don't know. It's still sitting in the box.

Please don't leave this training in the box. I don't care nearly as much about your reviews as I care about you taking action because I know that this method works. The lessons, the training, the techniques, the assessments – everything in this book is exactly the reason that I'm standing on the second floor of my own hostel writing this. We took over this place two months ago, and we're already in the middle of expanding. We tripled this business' revenue in two months, and we're going to hit 10x within the first year using the principles and techniques within this book.

I work with coaching clients, and I know these Rings work not just for me, but for you as well. If something doesn't work for you, or you get stuck, please ask in the Facebook group or email me. I'll answer you. I would love to hear your questions about what your first book should be about or what you should name your blog. I know it's hard to make that decision in a vacuum. Sometimes a small amount of guidance from someone who's just further down the path is all it takes to redirect you towards success.

I encourage you to go through the steps of this process, assess yourself, look at the barriers that have been holding you back and break through them. Look at the skill, assets, and tools you have available and begin to make a plan. Once you develop that plan, share it within the Facebook group. The power of the group is the supportive community. Someone will always write you words of encouragement, wisdom, and guidance based on their own experiences.

You don't have to go it alone. If I can give you one feeling right now, it's the feeling that you're part of a community. There is a group of people that would love to help you overcome those moments of self-doubt we all get.

My motto on my very first blog was, "Fortune favors the bold."[2] This is absolutely true. There are loads of people with brilliant ideas, business models, and pieces of knowledge that could change the world who take no action, and therefore receive no rewards. The world rewards the action-takers. The hesitaters get nothing.

You can be methodical and consistent – you don't have to be bold and scary. You don't have to burn all the boats behind yourself; consistent action following the same set of tasks day after day is how you build a business brick by brick. Consistency is how the tortoise beat the hare.[3] That's how you can build your dreams. More and more opportunities will come your way because people know they can rely on you to get things done.

I'm excited to see what you will accomplish. This is my favorite part of the book because the nitty-gritty is over. Now we're in the hope and excitement phase. If we can turn those barriers that held you back in the past into a feeling of hope and excitement, you've just become limitless. Your success will go from being a possibility to an inevitability. You have the ability to break through, and that gets me more excited than anything else.

Thank you so much for reading this book. I appreciate

that you spent time with me, which is your most valuable and precious resource. I believe in you. I know that you can succeed. If you have any questions, please reach out to me. This is the beginning of your journey. I can't wait to see you star in a story of great success.

# ONE LAST CHANCE

ServeNoMaster.com/break

Thank you for your purchase of Breakthrough. As an extra bonus, I want to give you FOUR additional free gifts. In additional to The Breakthrough Workbook, you will get:

## 1. Quit Your Job Checklist

The "Ready to Retire" checklist that lets you know the exact moment you can fire your boss forever. Mark the moment on your calendar when you can start living a life of freedom.

## 2. Author and Entrepreneur Accelerator - Lifetime Membership

Get lifetime access to the most powerful group you will ever join. As a permanent member of my private accelerator, you will get free content daily as well as support from thousands of others on the same path.

Every day there are new training videos, stories of success and moments of inspiration...all waiting for you.

## 3. Five Day Business Challenge - Complimentary Ticket

Each month, I run a challenge with interviews from 25 experts at building an online business. Together we will refine your online dreams and help you focus on the best path for YOUR life. At the end of the challenge, you will know the exact steps to take to break the chains to a job you no longer love.

## 4. Get My Next Book Free

Members of my tribe get complimentary review and beta reader access to my new books, before anyone else in the world knows. Get a chance to read my next book AND affect the final version with your suggestions and opinions.

.  .  .

You get these bonuses as well as a few surprises, when you enter your best email address below.

Accelerate your success and click the link below to get instant access:

ServeNoMaster.com/break

# FOUND A TYPO?

While every effort goes into ensuring that this book is flawless, it is inevitable that a mistake or two will slip through the cracks.

If you find an error of any kind in this book, please let me know by visiting:

ServeNoMaster.com/typos

I appreciate you taking the time to notify me. This ensures that future readers never have to experience that awful typo. You are making the world a better place.

# NOTES

## 1. Enemy at the Gates

1. www.bankrate.com/banking/savings/financial-security-0118/.
2. www.pittsburgh.cbslocal.com/2018/08/28/pittsburgh-enters-new-era-without-daily-printed-newspaper/.

## 3. What You Will Accomplish, Aka Unleash the Beast

1. www.law.com/2018/04/25/law-grads-hiring-report-job-stats-for-the-class-of-2017/?slreturn=20180731184118.
2. www.forbes.com/sites/prestoncooper2/2017/07/13/new-york-fed-high-lights-underemployment-among-college-graduates/#7d45a78a40d8.
3. www.cnbc.com/2018/02/15/heres-how-much-the-average-student-loan-borrower-owes-when-they-graduate.html.

## 4. What do You Want from Life?

1. www.johnaugust.com/2017/scriptnotes-ep-320-should-you-give-up-transcript.

## 12. Real Goals

1. www.innocenceproject.org/causes/eyewitness-misidentification/.

## 13. Accountability

1. Even if it isn't in the reflection questions section, you should write it down your answer in your Breakthrough Journal.
2. Solomon, P., Kubzansky, Philip E., Leiderman, P. Herbert, Mendelson, Jack H., Trumbull, Richard, & Wexler, Donald, Eds. (1961). Sensory Deprivation: A Symposium Held at Harvard Medical School. Cambridge, MA, Harvard University Press.

3.
www.ncbi.nlm.nih.gov/pmc/articles/PMC285801/pdf/pnas00159-0105.pdf.

## 14. Business is Not a Hobby

1. I'm a member of MENSA and only missed a single math question on the PSAT in high school. But I still hate spreadsheets.
2. I'll post a picture of him wearing this shirt on the Breakthrough page.
3. www.businessinsider.com/yahoo-could-write-off-entire-goodwill-value-of-tumblr-2016-2.
4. www.money.cnn.com/2017/06/13/technology/business/yahoo-verizon-deal-closes/.

## 19. The Glass Ceiling

1. www.youtube.com/watch?v=v-Dn2KEjPuc.
2. X is our task or desire, and Y is our problem, barrier, or excuse.

## 20. Psychological Barriers

1. *Sucker Punch Fight Club.*

## Psychological Barrier #1 - I'm too Dumb

1. www.psycnet.apa.org/record/1994-42029-001.
2. As explained in *Serve No Master* in great detail.

## Psychological Barrier #2 - Lack of Education

1. www.bls.gov/opub/reports/minimum-wage/2016/home.htm.
2. www.biography.com/people/dave-thomas-9542110.
3. www.ted.com/talks/ken_robinson_changing_education_paradigms.

## Psychological Barrier #3 - I Will Fail

1. William Shakespeare.
2. If it makes you feel better, they were no longer on active duty.
3. The answer is Richard Nixon, Ronald Reagan, and the first George

Bush.

4. Guess where I want you to write down your predictions and results?
5. www.economist.com/the-economist-explains/2016/06/19/why-weather-forecasts-are-so-often-wrong.
6. Paraphrased from Al Pacino in *Any Given Sunday*.
7. Turns out I was wrong again. After all their promises, they denied my claim for a sick child again.
8. Don't cheat. If you eat what the list tells you, that's not a prediction. Eat what you *want* to eat. Or make a prediction that you don't have the ability to cheat on.

## Psychological Barrier #4 - I Come From a Long Line of Losers

1. www.businessinsider.com/rags-to-riches-story-of-oprah-winfrey-2015-5.
2. www.gq.com/story/katt-williams-gq-profile-2018.

## Psychological Barrier #5 - It's Too Late

1. www.biography.com/people/colonel-harland-sanders-12353545.
2. www.independent.co.uk/news/obituaries/chaleo-yoovidhya-recluse-who-created-the-red-bull-energy-drink-7579362.html.
3. www.biography.com/people/laura-ingalls-wilder-9531246.
4. www.worldrecordacademy.com/sports/oldest_female_marathon_finisher_Gladys_Burrill_set_world_record_102023.html.
5. www.imdb.com/name/nm0000614/?ref_=fn_al_nm_1.
6. I hope you put the answer to this in your Breakthrough Journal. I shouldn't have to keep reminding you.

## Financial Barrier #1 - I'm Barely Getting By

1. www.cashfloat.co.uk/blog/technology-innovation/american-credit-card-changed-society/.
2. www.independent.co.uk/student/graduates-three-quarters-never-pay-off-debt-loan-maintenance-grant-institute-for-fiscal-studies-a7824016.html.
3. www.usatoday.com/story/money/personalfinance/2014/04/20/id-nv-ut-have-among-highest-payday-loan-rates/7943519/.

4. This is not a soft pitch to get a review from you. Most companies and marketers reward positive feedback.

## Financial Barrier #2 - Starting a Business is Expensive

1. In 2009, the Kaufman Foundation raised their estimate to $30,000.

## Financial Barrier #3 - The Banks Won't Loan Me Money

1. www.forbes.com/sites/forbestechcouncil/2018/06/15/silicon-valleys-secret-ingredient-to-startup-success/#7c97dd006049.

## Financial Barrier #4 - I'm in Debt

1. Unless you live in Las Vegas.

## Financial Barrier #5 - I Stink at Accounting

1. www.celebritynetworth.com/articles/entertainment-articles/rich-famous-get-ripped-off-business-managers-often-youd-think/.

## 25. Financial Barriers Activity

1. You can find more in-depth training and resources on the Breakthrough page of my website.

## Real-World Barrier #1 - My Entire Country is Poor

1. There are websites and apps dedicated to listing every place in the world where you can find free Internet access.

## Real-World Barrier #2 - I Work Two Jobs

1. I moved back in with my mom when I got started.

## Real-World Barrier #4 - I Went to Jail

1. Even Hitler's book is available on Amazon and has a high sales rank. No, I won't be linking to it.

## 39. The Shape of Water

1. Here is the entire quote for Bruce Lee enthusiasts.

    "Don't get set into one form, adapt it and build your own, and let it grow, be like water. Empty your mind, be formless, shapeless — like water. Now you put water in a cup, it becomes the cup; You put water into a bottle it becomes the bottle; You put it in a teapot it becomes the teapot. Now water can flow or it can crash. Be water, my friend."

    From the film *Bruce Lee: A Warrior's Journey.*

2. "The weight loss hasn't impacted my golf swing, but it may have screwed up my putting because now I don't have a nice cushion on my gut to rest my elbows."

    www.golf.com/tour-and-news/questions-john-daly.

## Asset One - Skills

1. And yes, if enough of you email me asking, I will post a video of me singing on the Breakthrough page.

## Asset Four - Gear

1. Unfortunately, the costumes were not public domain and, eventually, these videos disappeared.
2. I have three cameras that each cost around $100 back in 2010. They can still shoot killer video in HD.

## 51. The Expertise Perception

1. Most people are familiar with this quote from *Die Hard* but the original is from *Life of Alexander* by Plutarch. I bet you didn't think *Die Hard* would make it into this book twice!

## 53. Ring of Flame Reflection Questions

1. www.poetryfoundation.org/poems/43997/the-rime-of-the-ancient-mariner-text-of-1834.

## 57. The Content Creation Path

1. www.lofbomm.com.
2. This is for my book *Overcome Depression*. Feel free to listen to her sultry tones when you grab that book.
3. If you really want to know, she sounds like Kate Micucci.
4. I completed one year of the two-year program at ACX in Guildford. It's an awesome school for musicians, but I decided to get my MA in Applied Linguistics rather than complete a second undergraduate degree in recording bands.

## 58. The Arbitrage Path

1. Search engine optimization is the process of getting a website to rank at the top of search results. Today, that means ranking at the top of Google.
2. As happened to me with the sugar daddy social media site.
3. The rainmaker is the person who generates clients for a company.

## 59. The Made to Order Path

1. We can't use print on demand, as we would have to charge our guests triple for the same shirts, and it's hard to tell someone staying at your hostel for two nights that their shirt will be ready in about a week.
2. Two months later, and we haven't sold a single one. The designer messed up the color on all the shirts.
3. Use arbitrage to increase how many products you offer.
4. His first big product generated over a billion dollars in sales.

5. You can see the design on the Breakthrough page of my website.

## 60. The Rainmaker Path

1. Tier one is the person who introduces you to customers. Tier two is the person who introduces you to the tier-one people.
2. This isn't pyramid marketing, but there is no tier three, and you can't sell a product more than once.

## 61. The Affiliate Path

1. I have an awesome podcast breaking down the process of writing a review that makes you money. Listen to it.
2. The initial fees for recommendations like these will be small, but they are a great way to get a taste of making money doing what you would do anyways.
3. You can check out nearly any video game on metacritic to confirm these stats.
4. This happened to a video game reviewer named Jeff Gerstmann.
    www.forbes.com/sites/erikkain/2012/03/21/gaming-the-system-
    how-a-gaming-journalist-lost-his-job-over-a-negative-
    review/#4967fed54f25.
5. I put this into a lot of my books because I'm desperate to find a video game reviewer with a smidge of integrity. I only have an hour or two a week to play games, and I don't want to waste them playing something that stinks.

## 62. One Ring to Rule Them All

1. If you are an outlier, please email me your assessment, and I can help you find the right path for you.

## Conclusion

1. It was granted just two months later. Don't worry, I'm all legal now.
2. *Fortis fortuna adiuvat.* And yes, I know it's now the tattoo on John Wick's back, but Pliny the Elder said it first.
3. From Aesop's Fables.

# ABOUT THE AUTHOR

Born in Los Angeles, raised in Nashville, educated in London - Jonathan Green has spent years wandering the globe as his own boss - but it didn't come without a price. Like most people, he struggled through years of working in a vast, unfeeling bureaucracy.

And after the backstabbing and gossip of the university system threw him out of his job, he was "totally devastated" – stranded far away from home without a paycheck coming in. Despite having to hang on to survival with his finger-nails, he didn't just survive, he thrived.

In fact, today he says that getting fired with no safety net was the best thing that ever happened to him – despite the stress, it gave him an opportunity to rebuild and redesign his life.

One year after being on the edge of financial ruin, Jonathan had replaced his job, working as a six-figure SEO consultant. But with his rolodex overflowing with local businesses and their demands getting higher and higher, he knew that he had to take his hands off the wheel.

That's one of the big takeaways from his experience. Lifestyle design can't just be about a job replacing income, because often, you're replicating the stress and misery that comes with that lifestyle too!

Thanks to smart planning and personal discipline, he started from scratch again – with a focus on repeatable, passive income that created lifestyle freedom.

He was more successful than he could have possibly expected. He traveled the world, helped friends and family, and moved to an island in the South Pacific.

Now, he's devoted himself to breaking down every hurdle entrepreneurs face at every stage of their development, from developing mental strength and resilience in the depths of depression and anxiety, to developing financial and business literacy, to building a concrete plan to escape the 9-to-5, all the way down to the nitty-gritty details of teaching what you need to build a business of your own.

In a digital world packed with "experts," there are few people with the experience to tell you how things really work, why they work, and what's actually working in the online business world right now.

Jonathan doesn't just have the experience, he has it in a variety of spaces. A best-selling author, a "Ghostwriter to the Gurus" who commands sky-high rates due to his ability to deliver captivating work in a hurry, and a video producer who helps small businesses share their skills with their communities.

He's also the founder of the Serve No Master podcast, a weekly show that's focused on financial independence, networking with the world's most influential people, writing epic stuff online, and traveling the world for cheap.

All together, it makes him one of the most captivating and accomplished people in the lifestyle design world, sharing the best of what he knows with total transparency, as part of a mission to free regular people from the 9-to-5 and live on their own terms.

Learn from his successes and failures and Serve No Master.

*Find out more about Jonathan at:*
ServeNoMaster.com

## Develop Good Habits with S.J. Scott

How to Quit Your Smoking Habit

The Weight Loss Habit

## Seven Secrets

Seven Networking Secrets for Jobseekers

## Biographies

The Fate of my Father

## Complex Adult Coloring Books

The Dinosaur Adult Coloring Book

The Dog Adult Coloring Book

The Celtic Adult Coloring Book

The Outer Space Adult Coloring Book

The 2nd Celtic Adult Coloring Book

The Stop Smoking Adult Coloring Book

## Irreverent Coloring Books

Dragons Are Bastards

## Fiction

## Gunpowder and Magic

The Outlier (As Drake Blackstone)

# ONE LAST THING

Reviews are the lifeblood of any book and especially for the independent author. If you would click five stars on your eReader device or visit this special link at your convenience, that will ensure that I can continue to produce more books. A quick rating or review helps me to support my family and I deeply appreciate it.

Without stars and reviews, you would never have found this book. Please take just thirty seconds of your time to support an independent author by leaving a rating.

Thank you so much!

To leave a review on any platform go to ->

**https://servenomaster.com/breakthrough**

Sincerely,
Jonathan Green
ServeNoMaster.com

www.ingramcontent.com/pod-product-compliance
Lightning Source LLC
La Vergne TN
LVHW012200040326
832903LV00003B/27